PYTHON
DATA ANALYTICS

Comprehensive Guide of Tips and Tricks using Python Data Analytics Theories

ETHAN WILLIAMS

TABLE OF CONTENTS

Introduction

The large volumes of data are revolutionizing businesses across different industries in the world. Data analytics does not only play an essential role in a business, but it also plays a vital role in your life. For example, you can use data analytics to make better lifestyle choices or derive some information from a business to increase your profits. Since a business now collects real-time data, they need to understand how to use and analyze that data. This is where data analytics comes into picture.

Unfortunately, not many people are aware of what data analytics is and how they can analyze data. They often assume that business intelligence, analysis, algorithms, statistical analysis and statistical tools and software are very different, but in reality, they are interlinked. If you have been reading numerous articles across the Internet, you may be confused. If you are someone who works in the analytics team or wants to move to the analytics team, you should understand what data analytics is.

You can use this book as a guide to help you learn more about data analytics, python and how you can use python to develop algorithms for data analytics. Throughout the book, you will gather information on what data is, and how this data can be analyzed to obtain some information about the future. You will also learn more about what big data is and how you should analyze these large volumes of data. You will learn more about how you can perform an analysis using Python. This book also sheds some light on the different tools and algorithms that you can use for the same.

Thank you for purchasing the book. I hope you gather all the information you were looking for.

Chapter One

What Is Data?

The Webster dictionary defines data as a collection of information or facts that include numbers, measurements, words, observations, etc. This information and facts are fed as input data to the computer in a form that it can read. You know that data has changed the way the world makes decisions. There are numerous articles on the Internet that talk about how different companies use data to make informed decisions. These articles talk about how the company used data to boost its revenue, how doctors worked on developing a cure for a disease, how companies market their products to the right customers and more. Most of these articles refer to big data. This data is the volume of information that a human being and machine cannot read. Big data refers to the large volumes of information that are collected every minute of every day, and it is hard for human beings to read and understand this data.

Machine Versus Humans

Data that can be read by human beings, often unstructured data, is information that they can read, study and interpret. For example, human beings can understand the meaning of text and images in any form. If a human being can understand the data that is given to them, that information is termed as human-readable information. Structured or semi-structured data is termed as machine-readable information. This information refers to the information that a computer can read, understand and process. Computers process the information using scripts and programs. A program or script is a set of instructions written by a developer or coder. These instructions will make it easier for the computer to manipulate the data. A developer or data scientist can use this data to the right set of programs to develop a software.

Is The Position Of A Data Scientist The Best Job In The 21st Century?

Once this data is collected, it must be cleaned, processed, interpreted, analyzed and used in the right manner before the business or any human being can obtain insights. Regardless of the type of data that you look at or want to use, the person who performs the functions above is a data scientist. We will learn more about what data science is later in the book. The positions of a big data analyst and a data scientist are the most sought after positions in this century. Some believe that the job of the data scientist is the sexiest job in the world.

If you want to become a big data analyst or data scientist, you must have a basic understanding of statistics, modeling, analytics, math and computer science. The role of a data scientist is very different from a traditional job of a developer or modeler, because they need to understand numerous business processes. They are aware of how they should communicate their findings to the management and leaders to influence them to make the right decisions for the business.

Data Resources

This book will shed some light on data collection, big data, data science and how you can analyze that data to obtain some insights and make informed decisions. If you want to learn more about how you can analyze the data better and also learn from experts, you can use the resources mentioned in this section.

Data Blogs

- Nate Silver, a data wizard, runs the blog FiveThirtyEight. In this blog, Nate sheds some light on the different types of data analysis and also sheds some light on the different types of information and data that people use to obtain some insights about economics, sports, culture and politics.

- The Data Science Weekly is a blog that has all the information about any development in the field of big data analytics and data science.

- The blog Flowing Data has numerous visualizations, tutorials and resources that can be used to learn more about data analytics. This blog is run by Dr. Nathan Yau. This blog also provides some information on different humorous discussions and the different books that you can read to learn more about data analytics.

- KDnuggets is an online resource that has numerous articles and a lot of information about big data, data science, data analytics, machine learning, etc.

- Edwin Chen is a data scientist working at Dropbox, and he runs a blog that sheds some light on the different algorithms that can be used for analysis.

Chapter Two

Introduction to
Big Data and Big Data Analytics

Before we look at what data analytics is, let us look at what big data is and where this data is collected. The first few chapters of the book will shed some light on what big data is, what data analytics is and the different types of data analytics. It is only when you know what big data is and how you can analyze big data that you can move onto building tools that will help you in data analytics.

Big data analytics is the process of understanding and examining varied and large data sets. These large data sets are called big data and they are used to uncover some unknown correlations, hidden patterns, customer preferences and market trends. This data will help an organization make some informed decisions for the business. Data analytics techniques and technologies provide users to analyze large data sets and draw some conclusions about them. This will help the business make informed decisions. You can answer some business intelligence queries to improve the performance and operations of the business. Big data analytics involves the use of complex applications that include predictive models, what-if analysis and statistical algorithms. These applications are powered by analytics systems.

Importance of Big Data Analytics

As we read earlier, big data analytics is performed using specialized software and systems. This type of analytics offers numerous benefits, including:

- Competitive advantages over rivals

- More effective marketing

- Improved operational efficiency

- New revenue opportunities

- Better customer service

Predictive modelers, data scientists, statisticians, big data analysts and other analytics professionals use big data analytics applications to analyze the large volumes of structured data and other forms of data that are not tapped by other analytics or business intelligence programs. This data is a mix of unstructured and semi-structured data, including web server logs, Internet clickstream data, text from customer emails, survey responses, machine data and mobile content and social media content. This information is collected through some sensors connected to the IoT or Internet of Things. Big data analytics is a type of advanced analytics, which is very different from traditional business intelligence.

Big Data Analytics Tools and Technologies

Semi-structured and unstructured data types do not fit well into a data warehouse. These warehouses are based on relational databases that only work well with structured data sets. A data warehouse cannot handle processing demands posed by large volumes of data, especially when these data are frequently updated. This is the case with real-time data on online activities of visitors on a website, performance of mobile applications or stock trading.

As a result of this, numerous organizations have started to collect, process and analyze data, and they do this using Hadoop and NoSQL databases. They also use numerous data analytics tools like:

- MapReduce: This software provides a framework that allows a developer to write code or scripts to process large volumes of semi-structured or unstructured data across stand-alone computers or numerous processors.

- HBase: This tool is a value or key oriented data store that is built to run only on HDFC or Hadoop Distributed File System. The data in this tool can only be stored in the form of columns.

- YARN: This application can be looked at as the second-generation Hadoop, and is used to manage clusters in data sets.

- Pig: This is a technology that is open source, and also offers a high-level mechanism that allows parallel programing. It enables MapReduce to execute numerous applications or programs on Hadoop.

- Hive: This is a data warehouse system that is open source. It is used to query and analyze large data sets that are stored in Hadoop files.

- Spark: This tool provides analysts with a framework that enables them to process numerous scripts or programs in parallel. It also enables users to run a large-scale analytics application across numerous systems.

- Kafka: This tool is a messaging system that is designed to replace messaging systems used by brokers.

How Does Big Data Analytics Works?

NoSQL systems and Hadoop clusters are often used as the staging areas or landing pads for data before it is loaded into any analytical database or data warehouse for analysis and storage respectively. This data is loaded into these systems or clusters in a summarized form that is easier for the machine to understand, since it is in the same format as a relational database.

Big data analysts and users often adopt the concept of a data lake in Hadoop clusters. This data lake serves as the primary repository for any raw data that is collected by the system. The data is analyzed or run directly through a Hadoop cluster or Spark, a processing engine, respectively. Like every other data analysis process, it is important to remember that the data needs to be cleaned and processed when it is collected so it can be used for analysis. Any data being stored in HDFC should be cleaned, organized, configured and partitioned properly so it is easy for data analysts to extract, transform and load any analytical queries and integration jobs.

When the data is ready, a data analyst can analyze it using some commonly used software for some advanced analytics processes. These types of software include some tools for:

- Predictive analytics that helps analysts build models that can forecast any future developments or customer behavior

- Data mining which allows analysts to sift through large volumes of data to look for relationships and patterns in the data set

8

- Machine learning that allows analysts to use different statistical and mathematical algorithms to analyze large volumes of data

- Deep leaning which is an advanced form of machine learning

Some statistical analysis and text mining software also play an important role in the analytics process of big data. You can also use some data visualization tools and mainstream business intelligence software for the same. For both analytics and ETL applications, you can write queries in MapReduce using some programming languages like Scala, SQL, R and Python. These are the standard languages for relational databases that are supported on numerous Hadoop platforms.

Big Data Analytics Challenges and Uses

Every big data analytics application will use data from both internal and external sources like demographic data regarding customers, weather data and more. Some of this information can also be sourced from third-party applications or service providers. Additionally, some applications are being built to source real-time data so that analysts can perform real-time analytics on data that is fed into applications and cluster systems like Hadoop. This can only happen through stream processing engines like Storm, Spark and Flink.

Big data systems of the past were deployed based on the need of the organization. These organizations often collected, cleaned, organized, interpreted and analyzed large volumes of data. Microsoft, Amazon Web Services (AWS) and other cloud platform vendors have made it easier for organizations to set up and manage data in the cloud using Hadoop clusters. Suppliers of Hadoop like Cloudera-Hortonworks that supports the distribution of large volumes of data in Microsoft Azure and AWS cloud services. A user can now spin these clusters in the cloud, run them for as long as possible.

Supply chain analytics and businesses in other industries have begun to use big data analytics. In supply chain analytics, software uses both quantitative and big data methods to make it easier to process the data across the supply chain. Big data analytics in supply chain expands the data set, which allows the business owners to learn more from the data since they can improve their analysis. Some issues with big data analytics are that companies find it difficult to hire experience data engineers and scientists who can fill the gaps. Companies also find it difficult to analyze the data since the tools and software are expensive. Additionally, not every company has the right resources to perform some internal analysis.

The Emergence and Growth of Big Data Analytics

It was in the year 1990s that the term big data was used for the first time. This term was used to describe the large volumes of data being collected. Doug Laney, an analyst at Meta Group Inc., expanded the definition of big data. He ensured that people were aware that big data also includes a variety of data. This data is generated by large businesses frequently, and the speed at which this data is generated is unimaginable. This is when the three factors, called the important V's of big data, volume, variety and velocity were popularized.

Hadoop Distributed Processing Framework, HDFC, was launched as an open source project named Apache in the year 2006. This planted the seeds to build a clustered platform to run some big data applications. By the year 2011, most organizations began to look at big data analytics, and numerous applications like Hadoop and other big data technologies developed to cater to the increasing need.

Before the Hadoop ecosystem started and the framework began to mature, big data applications were taken care of by e-commerce and large Internet companies like Facebook, Yahoo and Google. This also included some marketing and analytical services that are required to interpret the data. Since financial service firms, retailers, healthcare organizations, energy companies, manufacturers, insurers and other enterprises have only started using big data analytics now to understand their customers better.

Chapter Three

Big Data Analytics

Big Data Analytics has gained immense popularity over the last few decades. Numerous stories have paved the way for the general public to be aware of the critical shortage of data scientists and also the Silicon Valley valuation bubbles. However, some concerns do emerge when you look at this topic in detail.

- Will Big Data replace the whole of my organization?

- Will the current investment in Business Intelligence go to waste?

- How can a Data Warehouse and Business Intelligence be used in tandem with Big Data?

- How soon can one show results when using Big Data Analytics?

- What skill sets are necessary to use Big Data Analytics?

- How does data governance get affected?

When you talk about Big Data Analytics with a large group of people, you will find two views that exist among the group – the first group worries about how this change will affect their business or their data privacy, and the second group is wondering how this change will benefit them. When it comes to any new field, especially with Big Data, it is important to strike a balance between both views to help create architecture that is robust and that accommodates both concerns.

What is Big Data? There are two sources of data that are often grouped under the Big Data Banner. The first source is the amount of data that is present within a corporation or business that is shared across a wide network. This information includes a blog, PDF documents, work documents, emails, business events, process events, and any other structured, semi-structured, or unstructured data that is available within the corporation. The second source of data is the data that is available outside the organization. Some of this information is available free of cost while there is some information that one would need to pay to obtain. This information is always accessible to the general public, but there is some information that is available to only certain members of the organization or certain customers. This information includes literature on products that are distributed by the competitors, information available on social media, hints from third parties, certain organization hierarchies, and also any complaints that may have been posted by customers on regulatory sites.

You may now ask what makes Big Data any different from any other data that has been used in the past. Four characteristics make Big Data significantly different from other types of data: volume, velocity, variety, and veracity. Other components separate Big Data from other data, but these are the most prominent.

Components of Big Data

Volume

Some organizations have already begun to struggle with the increasing sizes of their data warehouses as big data hit the world. It was mentioned in Fortune magazine that by the year 2003, that the world created digital data that was close to 5 exabytes. It was noted that this amount of digital data could be set up within two days in the year 2011. The time period is now expected to shrink to just a few minutes.

A few years ago, organizations used to count their data storage space for any analytics in terabytes. Now, they look at data storage space in petabytes. This data is causing a strain on the analytics infrastructure of some organizations in different industries. For instance, if you were to consider an organization that was in the communication industry, you would know that these would have at least 100 million customers. If data were collected for these clients on a daily basis, there would be at least five petabytes of data in a hundred days. Most companies try to get rid of data daily, but regulators have asked most businesses in the communication industry to store records about calls made or the data used by each customer.

Velocity

Velocity can be looked at from two perspectives – one representing latency while the other represents the throughput of data. Let us start with latency, which is one of the measures of velocity. Analytics was once a store-and-report environment where the data collected yesterday was often reported, and this was often represented as "D-1." Over the last decade, analytics has embedded itself into various business processes that gather data in motion, thereby reducing latency. For example, some advertising agencies are trying to conduct analytics to help them place advertisements on online platforms within 10 milliseconds.

Let us now look at the throughput of data, which represents the data moving in the pipes. The amount of global mobile data is said to be growing at a rate of 78% at a compounded rate, and the data collected is expected to reach 12 exabytes per month in 2017 as consumers and users begin to share more videos and pictures. To analyze this data, many corporations are seeking an analytical infrastructure that will help them process information in parallel.

Variety

In the late 1990s, when Data Warehouse technology was introduced, the initial idea was to create and represent data using meta-models that would help to represent all data collected in one format.

The data was often compiled from numerous sources and was transformed using ELT (Extract data, load it into the warehouse, and process the data within the warehouse) or ETL (Extract, Transform, Load). The basic idea was to narrow down the variety of data and then structure the content that was created. Big Data has helped to expand our horizons and has also contributed to enabling new data integration and analytics infrastructure and technology. Numerous call center analytics are seeking solutions that would assist them in analyzing the conversations that take place between customers and call center executives. The source data only includes unstructured text, video and sound, and some amount of structured data. Numerous applications are gathering their data from documents, blogs, or emails. For instance, Slice, a company used to provide analytics for online orders, uses raw data that comes from different organizations like online bookstore purchases, airline tickets, parking tickets, music download receipts, and any other purchases

15

that may have hit your email. How can this information be normalized into creating product catalogs and also analyzing any purchases made?

Another example that can be looked at is the InfoSphere Streams platform that was created by IBM. This platform has dealt with some sources for decision making and real-time analytics, including seismic data, medical instruments for neonatal analysis, network events, traffic patterns, CDRs, RFID tags, mainframe logs, weather data, video, and voices in different languages.

Veracity

Most internal data is carefully governed, while Big Data comes from sources outside the control of the company that often have some inaccuracies and incorrectness. Veracity represents the sustainability of data and also the credibility of the source of data for the target audience.

Let us look at how we can understand the credibility of the source. If organizations were to collect information on their products from third parties and provide it to their customers or contact center employees to help support customer queries, the organization would need to be screened and tested for accuracy and correctness. Otherwise, contact centers may end up recommending offers that may cause a reduction in the organization's revenue. Some social media responses to campaigns could come from disgruntled employees or customers of the company, which would impact the decisions made by the company. For instance, on a survey that is conducted by companies, a "like" would mean that the employees or customers were satisfied. However, what would happen if someone were to replace the "like" with something else?

We also have to look at how much truth can be shared with an audience. The veracity of any data collected or created within an organization is often assumed to be well intentioned. However, some or most of the data cannot be shared with the general public, which restricts wider communication. For instance, if customer service has provided the manufacturing and engineering department with the shortcomings of a particular product based on the feedback given by customers, the data shared should be selective and on a need-to-know basis only. Other data can be shared with some clients who have certain prerequisites or contracts.

Drivers for Big Data

The creation of Big Data has been rapidly increasing over the years. This section looks at the forces that drove the rapid creation of Big Data. Three factors majorly contribute to the establishment of Big Data – automation, monetization, and consumers. It is this interaction between these three forces that has increased the speed of creating Big Data.

When the automation of data increases, it is easier to offer Big Data creation and also improve the consumption opportunities of consumers, while the monetization process helps to provide an efficient market for Big Data.

Sophisticated Customers

The increase in the level of information available and the associated tools to work with that information has created a new set of sophisticated clients. These consumers are all experts at using technology and statistics, far more analytic and more connected to the world through social media than the customers from a decade ago. These clients know where to source the data from and what one can do with that data.

The world we live in is full of marketing messages, and while most marketing still happens in magazines, newspapers, radio, network TV, and even in conventional media, narrow casting of advertisements is gaining more popularity. This can be seen in the local ads in magazines, the insertion of commercials on set-top boxes, and the use of information from commuters to change the street display advertisements. The world of the Internet has become personalized. Electronic yellow pages, search engines, and social network sites all have ads that are unique to a particular segment of the public or an individual. Cookies on the Internet are all being used to track the behavior of the users and also create content based on the said behavior.

Text messages and emails have rapidly led to interpersonal interactions. Communication has not started with only marketers but has also started between friends and third parties and has expanded to group chats, bulletin boards, and social media, which would allow people to converse about their intentions and what they would like to purchase, their expectations, fears, and their disappointments with small and large groups. Unlike text messages and emails, a conversation that happens on the Internet is available for most people to read either now or later.

So far, we have only been looking at communication in a single form. Other sources combine all the information that is available in more than one media. For instance, Facebook conversations often involve some media, including sound clips, text, video, and photos. Alternative reality and second world information are both becoming exciting areas to try out product ideas in a world where product usage can be worked on and experimented with.

Most often, we need experts who would help us understand and sort out product features and how those features would relate to our usage of those products. Some experts are available to help us understand our usage, pricing, and quality and also provide us with valuable information on the products. Numerous marketers are encouraging ambassador or advisor programs using social media as their platform. These selected customers will always receive a preview of the new products that are being created and also actively participate in evaluating and promoting the product. It is true that the people we know and trust often sway the decisions we make. This is why social media is the biggest contributor to advertising and marketing. Social media has helped bring consumers together and has helped them share their experiences that assist them in making objective decisions about products.

Consumers form groups on social media and use different modes of communication – messages, emails, Facebook Messenger, Instagram, emails, and so on. It is always interesting to see how the leaders, consumers who lead the entire social group, sway the statistics.

There are numerous ways to utilize these social networks to influence reuse and purchase of these products.

Studying Consumer Experience

Most of the data collected is often unstructured. The data obtained from analyzing the text for intensity, sentiments, readership, referrals, related blogs, and any other information can be used to organize the data into negative and positive influences and also assess the impact of those influences on the consumer base.

Organizing Customer Experience

Numerous reviews can be provided to prospective consumers, which would help them evaluate the product they want to purchase.

Influencing Social Networks

Marketing material, company directions, product changes, and celebrity endorsements on social media would help control the likes and dislikes of prospective consumers.

Feedback on operations, marketing, or products

When organizations use information that is generated via social media, rapid changes can be made to the product mix to help improve how products are marketed to prospective consumers.

Society has played a significant role in the way the production process has been evaluated. However, the Internet and social networks have altered the access to information. A consumer could choose to "love" a product on Facebook, and every friend on the user's list would have instant access to this information. The same goes with every other social media platform.

Automation

Kiosks, Interactive Voice Response (IVR), email, mobile devices, chats, third- party applications, corporate websites, and social networks have helped generate a fair amount of information about the customers. In addition to this, the interaction that exists between consumers on different media can now be organized and analyzed. The biggest change lies in the organization's ability to modify the experience of customers using procedures, software policies, and personalization, which would make self-service customer friendly.

The sales and marketing departments in most organizations have received the biggest boost in instrumentation since they began to use Internet-driven automation. Shopping, browsing, ordering, and customer service on the Internet not only has provided users with tremendous control but has also created a massive flood of information to the product, marketing, and sales departments of the company to understand the behavior of a potential or existing buyer. Each sequence of clicks on the Internet can be collated, collected, and analyzed to understand a customer's delight, dysphoria, puzzlement, or even outright defection. A lot more information can be obtained using the sequence to understand the decisions that consumers make.

Self-service has started to creep in through different means: kiosks, IVRs, handheld devices, and numerous others. Each of these means of communications acts like a huge pool of time-and-motion studies. There is data that is available on the number of steps customers had taken, the products they have compared, and attributes that they focus on – price, brand, features, defects, comparisons, and so on.

Suppliers and retailers have obtained large amounts of data from the electronic sensors and self-service parts that are connected to the customer reactions to products. If a consumer uses a two-way set-top box at home, the supplier would have the ability to understand the channel surfing behavior of these users. Some questions can be answered through the data collected: Did the consumer change the channel when advertisements started? Did the user turn the volume down when a jingle began to play? When the user uses the Internet to shop for a product, the click stream can be used and analyzed to study his or her shopping behavior. How many products did the consumer look at? Did the user look at the product description or the price when he or she was watching the product? This set of data would help the supplier understand and analyze the consumer to the smallest detail.

What are the different sources of data that can be obtained from these self-service interactions?

Product

Products have started to become increasingly electronic and therefore provide a large amount of data to the supplier concerning the product and its quality. In most cases, suppliers are also able to collect information about how consumers are using a certain product. Products can also provide the suppliers with information on the frequency of use of the product, any interruptions, or any other related aspects.

Electronic Touch Points

Organizations can collect a large amount of data just by using certain touch points that are used to shop for products. The IVR tree traversals are often logged, which meant Web clicks could be collected and so on and so forth.

Components

At times, components help to provide additional information, which includes data about the failures of components, their uses, or the lack of those uses. For instance, a wireless CSP would help in the collection of data from various networks, third parties, cell towers or other handheld devices, which would help us to understand how components, when used together, would be good or bad for the customer.

Monetization

From the perspective of Big Data Analytics, it is possible to create a marketplace called a "data bazaar" where data can be collected and exchanged, as well as to help sell certain customer information. There is a new trend in the marketplace, in which the experience that certain customers have in one industry is anonymized, cleaned, packaged, and sometimes sold to other industries. Fortunately, Internet advertising helps to provide customers with an incentive to use services for free and certain opt-ins.

Internet advertising is a complex area. It has obtained revenue of over $30 billion, which goes to show that the industry is feeding a large amount of information to start-ups and also helps organizations with their initial public offering (IPO) activities. The most interesting part is that this advertising money contributes to enhancing the experience that customers have. Consider Yelp for instance – this website lets consumers share the experiences they have when they visit restaurants, nightclubs, malls, and spas, and it also understands their likes and dislikes when it comes to life and so on. Yelp obtains its revenue through advertising on its website, but most of the traffic that the website receives is from people who read other customer experiences that have been posted on the website. With this traffic reaching the Internet, some questions arise on how the usage of the Internet to capture experiences would help improve revenue for other companies.

Big Data Analytics helps to create a new market, which would help customers obtain data from one industry and also use it in another to help improve an organization's ability to increase their revenue.

Location

It was discussed earlier that the area is critical to suppliers because that would help them reach their target audience with ease. If it is assumed that a particular product is used with a mobile device, the location of the consumer would be critical, and this information would be helpful to the supplier.

23

Cookie

Most browsers carry a large amount of data using cookies. Some of this information could be directly associated with touch points.

Usage Data

A lot of data providers have begun to collect, categorize, synthesize, and pack information that can be used in the future, too. This would usually include credit-rating agencies that rate their customers, social networks with blogs that have been liked, and certain cable companies that would have some audience information. Some or maybe most of the data could be anonymized or be provided only in summary form.

Big Data Applications

This section discusses different uses of Big Data Analytics. In each of the cases mentioned in this section, Big Data Analytics has started to integrate with business processes and certain traditional analytics practices, which help to provide the main outcomes. In most cases, the uses would represent the game changers that are essential to the growth and survival of any organization in a competitive marketplace. Some of these applications could be still in their infancy, but there are others that have become very common.

Social Media Command Center

In the year 2014, Blackberry faced a serious crisis when the email servers used were down for more than a day. Most people had tried to turn on and turn off their Blackberry devices because they were unaware of whether or not it was an issue with the device or whether it was the CSP. Most people would never have thought about how this problem could have occurred on the Blackberry server. When most consumers called the CSP, they realized that the CSP had absolutely no idea about the issue.

It is a known fact that the VP of Blackberry is often glued to Twitter, looking for any problems faced by customers. Often, a problem with the server is identified on Twitter before the Internal monitoring team can even process the issue. There are some employees who are a part of the customer service team, marketing team, or the public relations team whose job is to look through social media for information. This does sound like an automation opportunity, does it not?

A social media command center often combines the feedback from most consumers using automated search and display on different social media. The feedback is most often summarized in the form of "negative" or "positive" sentiments. When the feedback is obtained, the marketer can always respond to the comments by entering into a conversation with the consumers affected either positively or negatively and then deciding whether or not they would need to respond to the questions or obtain feedback on new products. Through these conversations, they will be able to obtain automated solutions that would help the organization. The automated solutions are great at helping the consumer find information, categorize it based on the attributes, and also organize that information on dashboards, thereby orchestrating responses from consumers in a fraction of a second.

Product Knowledge Hub

When consumers begin to turn into sophisticated users of products and technology, and the marketplace becomes a specialized area for customers, product knowledge would rarely belong to only one organization. If you consider the iPhone, you will notice that although the product is marketed by Apple, the parts for the phone come from different suppliers, while the apps come from a community of app developers, and the communication services are provided by a CSP. Android, created by Google, is more diverse. Google only provides the operating system, but the cell phone manufacturers offer the device. Smartphones can never work in isolation. They can also act as Wi-Fi hubs for some other devices. What would happen when you want to tether your iPhone to an iPad? Would you call Apple for help? Or would you reach out to your service provider? Or would the website provide all the information you need?

The answer to these questions is based on three sets of technologies. The first part of the answer lies with the capability to tap into any source of data that is found. Most CSPs have pieces of the solution on their intranet that is put together by customer service subject matter experts or product managers. Some of the information could also come from a third party or a device manufacturer. This data would need to be pulled together and stripped of its control information so that raw text could be reused.

The second part is to be able to categorize the raw information using a set of indices that are created by the product manager. This also implies that the information can be found whenever needed. Given that there are some combinations of products that are in existence, it is important for organizations to collect and combine the information that is often searched on devices. The indexing system would help to organize the information to make it easily accessible.

The final part of the solution would involve creating an XML document against certain queries that could be rendered or created using a mashups engine, or it could be made available to third-party applications.

What is created is a product knowledge hub that would now be used from a website or distributed to different call centers. This would significantly help to reduce the call handling time in call centers and would also contribute to increasing the number of solutions provided on the first call. When this information is freely available on the Internet, it helps to promote CSP websites as a source of knowledge, which would increase the traffic on the Web, thereby reducing the number of people who would contact the call center about any problems they may have.

When a single source of knowledge has been created, the source could be used to upsell some products and also connect the useful knowledge to certain product features, thereby enhancing the knowledge pool to help discover newer goods and render business partnership ideas. A lot of fragmented and stray knowledge about the products could be used to find a variety of other uses for the product.

Infrastructure and Operations Study

Numerous industries are exploring the use of Big Data to help to improve their analytical infrastructure. Most often, the best way to explore these improvements is by attempting to understand the utilization of the infrastructure and how bottlenecks or any other configurations would impact performance. In the past, most data were manually collected, and this significantly increased cost to the organization. Big Data helps to provide a natural source of data without having to use people to collect the information by going from door to door.

Chapter Four

An Introduction To Data Science

Data science is a combination of algorithm development, technology and data inference. This discipline helps engineers and scientists solve some complex analytical problems. At the core of this analysis is data. As read earlier, there are troves of raw data that are streaming in. These data are stored in data warehouses, and there is so much one can learn from mining this data. The concept of data mining is covered later in the book. One can build many tools based on the inferences they make from data. Data science is how you can use this data to generate some value for the business or for yourself.

Data Insights

When you collect troves of information, you must know what to do with that information. When it comes to data science, it is all about uncovering some hidden information in the data. You must dive into the data and mine it to understand the behavior of different variables in the data set. When it comes to data science, it is all about surfacing the hidden information that will help companies make smarter business decisions. For instance, Netflix tracks every user's watching patterns and tries to understand what drives the user's interest. The business uses that information to decide what types of series or movies they should produce. Another example is Target. This company looks at the purchasing patterns of customers and looks for the major customer segments within that base. It then identifies the unique traits of that segment, and uses that information to guide the advertising to different audience bases.

So, how do data scientists mine insights? It all begins with data exploration. A data scientist must become a detective when they are giving a challenging question. They will investigate different leads and try to understand the characteristics or patterns within the data set. Once they identify these characteristics, the data scientist can choose to apply some quantitative or statistical techniques to understand the granularity of the data set. They can use techniques like segmentation analysis, synthetic control experiments, time series forecasting, inferential models, etc. The idea behind using these models is to understand what the data is trying to say. This insight is central to providing some strategic guidance. In this sense, data scientists act like guiding business stakeholders or consultants to find something within the data.

Development of Data Products

Data products are technical assets that collect data, utilize that data and process that data to return some results. These results are generated through some algorithms. A classic example is a recommendation engine. This data product uses user data to generate some personalized recommendations. These recommendations are based on that data. Let us look at some examples:

- The spam filter used in Gmail is a data product. This product uses an algorithm to process incoming mails. It will then determine if that email is junk or not.

- Another data product is the computer vision used in self-driving cars. This product uses some machine learning algorithms to recognize pedestrians, cars and objects on the road, traffic lights, etc.

- Amazon also uses a data product to suggest to its customers the different products they should buy.

This is very different from the section above where data scientists look for data insights alone. Here, the outcome is to provide some advice to the business so it can make a smart business decision. In contrast to this, a data product is a technical functionality. This product will encapsulate an algorithm and is designed to fit directly into the application. Data scientists play a key role in developing a product. This will involve building an algorithm, testing it, refining it and deploying that algorithm into the production system. A data scientist works as a developer to building assets.

Chapter Five

Big Data Analytics Vs. Data Science Vs. Data Analytics

This chapter will cover some of the differences between data science, big data, and data analytics.

Data Analytics

The science of collecting, processing, and analyzing raw data to draw analyses or conclusions from that information is known as data analytics. This field involves the application of a mechanical or algorithmic process that will help the analyst or user derive some insight from the data. For instance, you can run many data sets through a process that will help you identify a meaningful correlation between the datasets.

Data analytics is used in different fields and industries and allows companies and organizations to make informed decisions about their businesses. They can also use different tools to verify or disprove some existing models and theories. The focus of this type of science lies only in inference. The inference is the process of obtaining the conclusions based on the data and what the analyst knows.

Big Data

Earlier, data was collected using some applications or methods since there was only so much that one had to collect. Now, data is being collected every second of every day, which makes it hard to use traditional applications and methods to collect that data. This data, because of its large volume, is known as big data. When it comes to Big Data, you have to first start with the raw data that is not yet cleaned or collated. It is also impossible to store all that information on the computer because of the volume of the data.

From the previous chapter, you know that data can be collected from any device or person. This data can be structured, unstructured, and semi-structured, and the volume of this data overwhelms a business on a day-to-day basis. An analyst or business owner can use this data to analyze and derive insights from the data, which will lead to better strategic business moves and decisions. Gartner said that big data is high velocity, wide variety and high-volume information that demands cost-effective and innovative forms of processing, which provide enhanced decision making, process automation, and insight.

Applications of Data Science, Data Analytics and Big Data

This section covers some of the applications of data science, data analytics, and big data.

Data Science

Internet Search

Most search engines use data science algorithms to deliver the best results when someone looks for a query in a nanosecond or less.

Digital Advertisements

Every organization, big or small, in the digital marketing industry, always uses some data science algorithm to develop digital billboards and display banners. Digital advertisements receive more responses when compared to traditional advertisements for this reason.

Recommender Systems

Recommender systems make it easy for an individual to find the right product from the massive volume of products available. These systems also improve user-experience. Many companies use this system to promote their products based on the user's wants and demands. These suggestions are always based on the user's previous searches and purchases.

Big Data

Financial Services

Retail banks, credit card companies, insurance firms, private wealth management advisories, institutional investment banks, and venture funds always use big data for the financial services that they provide. The issue with these is that each of these organizations uses massive volumes of data that have many categories. Therefore, big data is used in the following ways:

- Compliance Analysis
- Customer Analysis
- Operational Analytics
- Fraud Analytics

Communications

Retaining customers, gaining new subscribers, or expanding within the current base are the top priorities for most telecommunication service providers. The solutions to all these challenges lie only in the ability to analyze and combine the massive volumes of customer and machine-generated data, which is created every single day.

Retail

Regardless of whether you own a retail or online store, the only way you can stay in the game is by understanding what your customers want, and how you can serve them better. This will require you to have the ability to analyze different types of data from a variety of sources. These sources include customer transaction data, weblogs, social media, loyalty program data, and store-branded credit card data.

Data Analysis

Healthcare

Like every organization, a hospital also has issues with cost and always looks for ways to minimize cost. The challenge here is that the hospital must learn to cut or tighten costs while it treats the maximum number of patients and improves the quality of patient care. Hospitals now use machine and instrument data to optimize and track treatment, patient flow, and the equipment that the hospital uses. Experts have said that there will be a one percent gain in efficiency if hospitals continue to use this data. This means that hospitals can globally save $63 billion.

Travel

Through data analytics, companies can optimize and enhance the buying experience of their customers through the data they obtain from social media and weblog data analysis. Many travel sights try to gain insights into their customers' preferences and desires using data analytics. They can upsell their products by correlating user preferences with the current sales. They identify user preferences by following their customer's browsing. This allows companies to create customized offers and packages.

Gaming

Companies developing games can collect the following data and use that data to optimize and enhance the user experience within the game:

- Likes and dislikes of the customer
- What types of games did the customers prefer buying?
- Relationships that the customer shares with characters in the game

Energy Management

Firms use data analytics to manage the consumption of energy. This includes energy optimization, smart-grid management, building automation, and energy distribution in utility companies. The applications or algorithms are centered on the monitoring and controlling of dispatch crews, manage service outages and network devices. An engineer can use the millions of data points present in the utility network and monitor the use of energy.

Skills Required

Data Science and Data Analytics

Programming Languages

Regardless of what role you are interviewing for, you are expected to learn to use some statistical programming languages like Python, R, and query languages like SQL. These are important to know since they are considered the tools of the trade.

Statistics

You must have a good understanding of the subject. You must be aware of the different tests, methods, distributions, probability, and maximum likelihood estimators. You must know these concepts well since they will help you understand and analyze data better. The trick is to identify the right method to use for different data sets. Data-driven companies use statistics to understand their customers and also to make decisions that will benefit the company.

Machine Learning

If you work in a large company that uses big data or large volumes of data or is working at a data-driven company like Uber, Google Maps, and Netflix, you must understand what machine learning is and its different learning methods. Most techniques that are implemented to help a machine learn can be implemented using Python or R. Therefore, and it does not necessarily mean that you need to know how the algorithms work. You do not have to build machine learning models, but you must understand what machine learning is at a basic level.

Linear Algebra and Multivariate Calculus

One must understand these concepts, especially if you are working in a company that is defined by data. This is because any improvement made to the algorithm will help in predicting outcomes that will help in improving the status of the company. You may be asked to derive or obtain some results using statistical methods during the interview. You may wonder why a data scientist will have to understand these concepts when one can use R or Python for the same. The answer is that it is best to learn these concepts so a data scientist can implement these concepts in their work without having to use R or Python.

Data Wrangling

The data that is being analyzed is often tricky to work with and can be messy. Therefore, it becomes crucial to know how one can deal with any imperfection in the data. These imperfections are essential to note, and you should master this skill regardless of which company you are working for.

Data Communication and Visualization

It is crucial for you to build this skill, especially if you own or work for a young company, which uses data to make decisions for the future. This skill is also useful in companies where the data scientist is viewed as a person who helps the company and other employees of the company make informed decisions. Concerning communication, you will need to represent your findings and also describe it to a broad audience. You can use visual aids like graphs and charts to enhance your communication.

Software Engineering

If you are being interviewed for a new company, and are the first data scientist to be interviewed, it is essential that you learn some software and also learn how to build code. This is because you will be working on developing new products.

Data Intuition

Companies always want to know if you are someone who can solve problems. You have to think of how you will be working with data engineers, product managers, and employees to understand data. Indeed, you cannot base all your analyses on your intuition, but you must understand what it is that you should do with the data.

Big Data

Analytical Skills

You must have the ability to make sense of the volumes of data that you have and work with. You should also ensure that you use your analytical skills to identify a relevant solution to a problem.

Creativity

You must have the ability to create and develop new methods that will help you interpret, collect, and analyze any strategy. This skill is essential for one to possess.

Business Skills

Every big data professional must understand business objectives and the processes that drive the growth of the business.

Apart from these skills, a big data professional must also know mathematics and statistics and should be well versed in some programming languages.

Tips and Tricks

Now that we know what data science, data analytics, and big data are, let us look at some tips that will help you make it in the world of data science. This section gives you some pointers and also enables you to understand how to face interviews and when the right time is to jump to a different company.

- When you want to become a data scientist, analyst, or big data professional, there are some steps that you will need to follow to ensure that you achieve your aim.
- Brush up on your statistics and mathematics skills as a data scientist, analyst, or big data professional, analyst and big data professional must know what the data is trying to tell

them. To do that, you will need to understand statistics and probability. You may need to learn advanced mathematics for some positions, but this is the best place to start.

- Understand what machine learning is and the different types of learning like supervised, unsupervised, and reinforcement learning.

- Learn how to code. Data scientists, analyst, or big data professionals need to learn languages like R and Python to teach the computer to analyze data.

- Understand what databases are and how data can be stored. It is important to understand how databases are built since it is vital to learn how to build those repositories. This will help you identify the big picture.

- Learn how to clean and munge the data. The latter is a process that converts raw data to a format that is easy for the data scientist, analyst, or big data professionals to analyze. The former is a method that is used to remove duplication and data that hampers the analysis. These tools are essential for a data scientist, analyst or big data professional to possess.

- Understand how important it is to visualize and report data. You do not have to become a graphic designer, but you must understand how to create reports that a layperson will understand.

- Gain expertise and learn more tools only once you have mastered the skills above. It would be best to learn other programming languages and also learn new ways to analyze data. It is this extra learning that will set you apart from your competitors.

- You must practice how to use data science to analyze and interpret data. You can do this by developing your data source and work with other data scientists, analyst, or big data professionals. It is always better to have some work that you can show to your interviewer.

- Follow the leaders in the data science industry and read their blogs to understand and learn more about data science. This will help you stay abreast with new theories.

Chapter Six

Types of Data Analytics

Businesses and other devices collect information every second from different parts of the world. It becomes imperative to have tools that will help us with the amount of data that is being generated. If data is in the raw format, it is unstructured and often not very useful to anyone. There is a lot of vital information that can be derived from structuring raw data. That is where data analysts come into the picture. This is also where different types of data analytics come into the picture. Businesses can drive new initiatives when they have insights available, which are driven by data.

The required analysis and workflow give rise to the four most important types of data analytics. They are as follows.

- Descriptive analytics

- Prescriptive analytics

- Diagnostic analytics

- Predictive analytics

Let us try to understand each of these one by one and when precisely these are employed.

Descriptive Analytics

Simply put and understood by the name itself, descriptive analytics is a process where raw data extracted from various sources is converted into a summarized form that can be understood by humans easily. The process results in describing an event from the past in great detail. Descriptive analytics can help derive patterns from past events and also help draw interpretations from those events, eventually assisting an organization in to frame and create better strategies for the future. It is the most commonly employed analytics across most organizations. Measures and key metrics can be revealed with the help of descriptive analytics in almost any kind of business.

Prescriptive Analytics

The process of breaking down the data step by step in a given situation is what is known as prescriptive analytics. For example, consider that you have booked a cab on Uber. The Uber driver is on his way to pick you up, but the regular route has a lot of traffic on it. He then gets an alternate route shown to him on Google Maps. This is a part of prescriptive analytics. Google Maps analyzed the current situation and suggested an alternative route to the Uber driver so that he reaches you for a pick up as soon as possible, and time is not wasted. This leads to a better customer experience, as well.

Diagnostic Analytics

Diagnostic analytics is known as the successor of descriptive analytics. With the help of diagnostic analytics, data scientists can dig deeper into a problem and eventually reach the source of that problem. The tools used for descriptive analytics and diagnostics analytics usually go hand in hand in any business environment.

Predictive Analytics

A business needs to have foresight and vision if it wants to succeed. Predictive analytics helps businesses to forecast patterns and trends by analyzing present-day events. From predicting the probability of events that might take place in the future or even trying to estimate the exact time that the event will take place, it can all be forecasted using predictive analytics. Predictive analytics makes use of variables that are co-dependent to create a pattern and understand the ongoing trend. For example, if you look at the healthcare domain, based on an individual's current lifestyle, which consists of his/her eating habits, exercise, travel time, etc. you can predict the kind of illnesses they are likely to contract in the future. Therefore, it can be said that predictive analytic models are the most important as they can be employed across all fields of life. We will look at this in further detail in the later chapters of the book.

Chapter Seven

An Introduction To Python
Running Python

You can run Python on numerous operating systems, including Unix, Windows, Linux, and Mac OS X or OS/2. The Python software is installed in your system. Python is already installed in your system if you use the GNU/Linux or Mac OS X operating systems. Experts suggest that you use this type of system since Python is already set up the programs in this bookwork on any operating system.

Installing on Windows

If you use Windows, you will first need to install Python, after which you will need to configure some settings. Ensure that you do this before you begin to use the codes in this book. To make the necessary changes, you will need to check the instructions provided for your operating system and follow them word for word. You can use the following pages for the same:

- http://wiki.Python.org/moin/BeginnersGuide/Download

- http://www.Python.org/doc/faq/windows/

- http://docs.Python.org/dev/3.0/using/windows.html

The first step is to download the authorized installer. Other kinds for Itanium machines and AMD can be accessed at http://www.Python.org/download/. This file, which has a .msi extension, must be saved at a location that you can find easily. You should then click on the Python installation wizard. This will take over the installation process. Always use the recommended settings until you know what changes you need to make.

Installing on Other Systems

You can install Python on other systems as well. The instructions for Unix-like and Linux systems can be found at the following links:

- http://docs.Python.org/dev/3.0/using/unix.html

If you are using the OS X, follow the instructions given below:

- http://www.Python.org/download/mac/

- http://docs.Python.org/dev/3.0/using/mac.html

Choosing the Right Version

Different installers include different numbers after the word Python, which refers to the version number. If you look at the archives on multiple websites, the version numbers will range from 2.5.2 to 3.0, where the former is an old but usable version of Python while the latter is the latest version. The Python team released version 2.6 at the same time that it released version 3.0. Some programmers may choose this because they may want to use the old version of Python but still make use of the new features of the latest version.

Python is continuously evolving, and the latest version of this software is version 3.1.1. You must keep in mind that these new versions are the same as version 3.0 with some refinements.

Therefore, the newer versions will continue to be referred to as 3.0 in this book. Version 3.0 includes several changes to the programming language that is incompatible with version 2.0. You do not have to worry about programming using different versions of Python since there is only a subtle difference in the language or syntax.

Python may run differently on different operating systems, but we will not be covering that aspect since that is outside the scope of this book. The codes in the book will work in the same way across different operating systems. This is one of the many good points of Python. If you wish to learn more about Python, you should read the documentation prepared by the developers, which are free and well written. It is available at http://www.Python.org/doc/.

Getting Started

When you sit down to write a new program, you must remember that it starts with a problem.

Before you write code for anything, you have to develop an idea of what it is that you would like to create and the problem that you are looking to solve. This will help you develop a fair idea of how you would like to solve the problem.

Throughout the next chapter, we will look at the software development cycle, which will help you through the process of designing the software. This is a step that most people will need to learn separately since most programming guides usually switch to the intricacies of the language and focus on how to develop code. This will make it difficult for a beginner to understand how to understand the code and what needs to be done to fix that code.

Understanding the principles of software design can dramatically speed up the process of creating new software and help ensure that important details are not missed out.

In the subsequent chapters, you will learn to build the designs and ideas in Python and learn to construct the basic units of the codes using words, data, and numbers. You will also learn how to manipulate these inputs to refine the code. It is important to learn how to compare different sets of data to make informed decisions. Throughout the book, you will learn to refine the designs you have created and break them down into portions that can be coded easily. These steps will help to expand your understanding of the language and help you turn your ideas into complete computer programs.

Creating your Files

Python is described as a self-documenting language, which does not mean that the user manual is written for you by Python. However, you can add documentation strings, which are defined as blocks of text, to your script or code. These documentation strings will show up when you open your code, which can then be turned into web pages that provide useful references to those looking for similar code. An example of documentation strings has been provided in the subsequent chapters, and it is important to learn to include documentation strings in your code at an early stage.

In the last chapter, we learned that an identifier is a part of a variable, which is a unit of data. These variables and identifiers are held in the computer's memory, and its value can be changed by modifying a value that is already present in the variable. This chapter will introduce you to the different types of variables that you can use when writing a program in Python. You will also learn how these variables can be used to convert your designs into working codes using Python. This is when you begin real programming.

Throughout this chapter, we will work on two programs – one where we will learn to format and manipulate text strings and another to perform a simple mathematical calculation.

The programs mentioned above can be written easily using different variables. When you use variables, you can specify a function, method of calculation that must be used to obtain a solution without the knowledge of the type of value that the variable must refer to in advance. Every piece of information that must be put into a system needs to be converted into a variable before the interpreter uses it in the function. The output of the program is obtained once the interpreter runs the contents or the values of the variables through the functions in the program.

Chapter Eight

Data Types and Variables

The previous book shed some light on what Python is and how you can use Python for analytics. You learned more about the different techniques of data analytics, like data visualization. The next few chapters will help you understand the basics of Python so you can work on developing your very own models.

This chapter will introduce you to the different types of variables that you can use when writing a program in Python. You will also learn how these variables can be used to convert your designs into working codes using Python. This is when you begin real programming. Throughout this chapter, we will work on two programs – one where we will learn to format and manipulate text strings and another to perform a simple mathematical calculation.

The programs mentioned above can be written easily using different variables. When you use variables, you can specify a function, method of calculation that must be used to obtain a solution without the knowledge of the type of value that the variable must refer to in advance. Every piece of information that must be put into a system needs to be converted into a variable before it can be used in a function. The output of the program is only received when these variables are used as parameters in functions.

Choosing the Right Identifier

Every section of your code is identified using an identifier. The compiler or editor in Python will consider any word that is delimited by quotation marks, has not been commented out, or has escaped in a way by which it cannot be considered or marked as an identifier. Since an identifier is only a name label, it could refer to just about anything. Therefore, it makes sense to have names that can be understood by the language. You must ensure that you choose a name that has not been used in the current code to identify any new variable.

If you choose a name that is the same as the older name, the original variable becomes inaccessible. This could be a bad idea if the name were chosen as an essential part of your program. Luckily, when you write a code in Python, it does not let you name a variable with a name used already. The next section of this chapter lists out the important words, also called keywords, in Python, which will help you avoid the problem.

Python Keywords

The following words, also called keywords, are the base of the Python language. You cannot use these words to name an identifier or a variable in your program since these words are considered the core words of the language. These words cannot be misspelled and must be written in the same way for the interpreter to understand what you want the system to do. Some of the words listed below have a different meaning, which will be covered in later chapters.

- False

- None

- Assert

- True

- As

- Break

- Continue

- Def

- Import

- In

- Is

- And

- Class

- Del

- For

- From

- Global

- Raise

- Return

- Else

- Elif

- Not

- Or

- Pass

- Except

- Try

- While

- With

- Finally

- If

- Lambda

- Nonlocal

- Yield

Understanding the Naming Convention

Let us talk about the words that you can use and those you cannot use. Every variable name must always begin with an underscore or a letter. Some variables can contain numbers, but they cannot start with one. If the interpreter comes across a set of variables that begin with a number instead of quotation marks or a letter, it will only consider that variable as a number. You should never use anything other than an underscore, number, or letter to identify a variable in your code. You must also remember that Python is a case-sensitive language. Therefore false and False are two different entities. The same can be said for vvariable, Vvariable and VVariable. As a beginner, you must make a note of all the variables you use in your code. This will also help you find something easier in your code.

Creating and Assigning Values to Variables

Every variable is created in two stages – the initialization and assignment of a value to that variable. In the first step, you must create a variable and name it appropriately to stick a label on it, and in the second step, you must put a value in the variable. These steps are performed using a single command in Python using the equal to sign. When you must assign a value, you should write the following code:

Variable = value

Every section of the code that performs some function, like an assignment, is called a statement. The part of the code that can be evaluated to obtain value is called an expression. Let us take a look at the following example:

Length = 14

Breadth = 10

Height = 10

Area_Triangle = Length * Breadth * Height

Any variable can be assigned a value or an expression, like the assignment made to Area_Triangle in the example above.

Every statement must be written in a separate line. If you write the statements the way you would write down a shopping list, you are going the right direction. Every recipe begins in the same way with a list of ingredients and the proportions and the equipment you would need to use to complete your dish. The same happens when you write a Python code – you first define the variables you want to use and then create functions and methods to use on those variables.

Recognizing Different Types of Variables

The interpreter in python recognizes different types of variables – sequences or lists, numbers, words or string literals, Booleans and mappings. These variables are often used in Python programs. A variable called None has its own called NoneType. Before we look at how words and numbers can essential in Python, we must first look at the dynamin typing features in Python.

Working with Dynamic Typing

When you assign a value to a variable, the interpreter will choose to decide the type of value the variable is, which is called dynamic typing. This type of typing does not have anything to do with how fast you can type on the keyboard. Unlike the other languages, Python does not require that the user declare the types of variables being used in the program. This can be considered both a blessing and a curse. The advantage is that you do not have to worry about the variable type when you write the code, and you only need to worry about the way the variable behaves.

Dynamic Typing in Python makes it easier for the interpreter to handle unpredictable user input. The interpreter for Python accepts different forms of user input to which it assigns a dynamic type, which means that a single statement can be used to deal with numbers, words, or other data types. The user does not always have to know what data type the variable must be. Since you do not have to declare a variable in Python before you use it, you may be tempted to introduce a new variable somewhere in the code. You must remember that you will never receive an error from Python until you use a variable that does not have a value assigned to it. That being said, it is very easy for a programmer to lose track of the variables being used and where the variables are set up in the script. You can choose to perform two different functions if you want to avoid these issues. You will need to use these techniques, especially when you begin to create numerous variables in your script. The first option is to bunch all the variables at the start of the code. You can also assign some default values to these variables. The next option is always to maintain a record of the different variables you are creating. You can do this by maintaining a data table in the comments or documents that you write for each program.

Python will always need to keep track of the variables that you include in the script. The first is that the machine will need to save some memory to store the value in the variable. It is important to remember that every data type takes up different amounts of space. The second is that when you keep track of the different variables, you can avoid making errors in your code. Python will flag an error called TypeError if you operate on a variable that does not support that operation. This may seem irritating at first, but this is one of the most useful features of the language. Let us look at the example below:

```
>>> b = 3

>>> c = 'word'

>>> trace = False

>>>
```

b + c

Traceback (most recent call last):

File "", line 1, in <module>

TypeError: unsupported operand type(s) for +: 'int' and 'str'

>>> c - trace

Traceback (most recent call last):

File "", line 1, in <module>

TypeError: unsupported operand type(s) for -: 'str' and 'bool'

The program above tries to operate data types that are incompatible. You cannot remove the Boolean answer yes/no or add any number to a text variable. You must always convert the data type before you to try to process it. It is important to convert the data type to another type that is compatible with the operation. You can combine words or numbers as you would normally, but you cannot perform an arithmetic operation on a text data type. Python will throw an alert, called the TypeError, which will help you trace the error in the script that you have written. The error will tell you where the error is in the code and will point you to the exact line. You can then work on giving the code clear instructions so you can get the required value from the equation.

A data type is used to help you represent any information that can be found in the real world. What I mean by the real world is the world that exists outside the computer. In the previous examples, we used the data types int and str. You will soon learn that these data types can only be used to indicate the most uncomplicated information.

You can combine these data types to develop some complex data types. We will cover this a little later in the book. You will first need to learn more about the building blocks that you can use to define the data and also identify the set of actions that you would like to perform to manipulate the values held by these variables.

The None Variable

A predefined variable called None is a special value in Python. This variable has its value and is useful when you need to create a variable but not define or specify a value to that variable. When you assign values such as "" and 0, the interpreter will define the variable as the str or int variable.

Information = None

A variable can be assigned the value None using the statement above. The next few examples will use real-world information that will be modeled into a virtual form using some fantasy characters. This example uses some statistics to represent some attributes of the characters to provide data for the combat system. You can use this example to automate your database and your accounts. So, let us take a look at some of the characters in the example.

In the program, hello_world.py, you saw how you could get a basic output using the print () function. This function can be used to print out the value of the variable and a literal string of characters. Often, each print statement must start on a new line, but several values can be printed on a single line by using a comma to separate them. You can use print () to concatenate all the variables into a single line only separated by spaces.

>>> Race = "Goblin"

```
>>> Gender = "Female"

>>> print (Gender, Race)
```

Female Goblin

Different segments of information can be combined into a single line using multiple methods. Some of these methods are more efficient when compared to others. Adjacent strings that are not separated will be concatenated automatically, but this is not a function that works for most variables.

```
>>> print ("Male" "Elf")
```

The expression above will give you the following output – "MaleElf"

When you enter the following code,

```
>>> print ("Male" Race)
```

You will receive the following error:

```
File "<stdin>", line 1

print ("Male" Race)

              ^

SyntaxError: invalid syntax
```

This approach cannot be used since you cannot write a string function as a variable and a string together since this is just a way of writing a single line string.

Using Quotes

In Python, a character is used to describe a single number, punctuation mark, or a single letter. A string of characters used to display some text is called a string or string literal. If you need to tell the interpreter that you want a block of text to be displayed as text, you must enclose those characters in quotation marks. This syntax can take multiple forms –

'A text string enclosed in single quotation marks.'

"A text string enclosed in double quotation marks."

"'A text sting enclosed in triple quotation marks.'"

If the text is enclosed in quotes, it is considered the type str (string).

Nesting Quotes

There are times when you may want to include literal quotation marks in your code. Python allows you to include a set of quotation marks inside another set of quotation marks if you use a different type of quotation mark.

>>>text= "You are learning 'how to' use nested quotes in Python."

In the example above, the interpreter will assume that it has reached the end of the string when it reaches the end of the text at the second set of double quotes in the string above. Therefore, the substring 'how to' is considered a part of the main string, including the quotes. In this way, you can have at least one level of nested quotes. The easiest way to learn how to work with nested quotes is by experimenting with different types of strings.

>>> boilerplate = """

```
#===(")===#===(*)===#===(")===#

Egregious Response Generator

Version '0.1'

"FiliBuster" technologies inc.

#===(")===#===(*)===#===(")===#

"""


>>> print(boilerplate) #=== (") ===#=== (*) ===#=== (")
===#

Egregious Response Generator

Version '0.1'

"FiliBuster" technologies inc.

#===(")===#===(*)===#===(")===#
```

This is a useful trick to use if you want to format a whole block of text or a whole page.

How to use Whitespace Characters

Whitespace characters are can often be specified if the sequence of characters begins with a backslash. '\n' produces a linefeed character that is different from the '\r' character. In the output window, the former would shift the output to a new line, while the latter would shift the output to a new paragraph. You must understand the difference between how different operating systems use to translate the text.

The usage and meaning of some of the sequences are lost on most occasions. You may often want to use \n to shift to a new line. Another useful sequence is \t, which can be used for the indentation of text by producing a tab character. Most of the other whitespace characters are used only in specialized situations.

Sequence	Meaning
\n	New line
\r	Carriage Return
\t	Tab
\v	Vertical Tab
\e	Escape Character
\f	Formfeed
\b	Backspace
\a	Bell

You can use the example below to format the output for your screen:

```
>>> print ("Characters\n\nDescription\nChoose your character\n \
\tDobby\n\tElf\n\tMale\nDon\'t forget to escape \'\\\'."
)
```

Characters

Description

Choose your character

> Dobby

> Elf

> Male

Don't forget to escape '\.'

You must remember that strings are immutable, which means that they cannot be changed. It is possible to use simple functions to create new strings with different values.

Converting Data Types

Different built-in functions are used in Python to convert a value from one data type to another. The data types often used are:

- int (x) – used to convert any number into an integer

- float (x) – used to convert a number to a float data type

- str (object) – convert any type into a string that can be used to print

>>> float (23)

23.0

>>> int (23.5)

23

>>> float (int (23.5))

23

Chapter Nine

Conditional Statements

In the last few chapters, you have learned how to use Python to manipulate strings and to make simple calculations. More importantly, you have learned how to design your software. Now, it is time to learn how to refine your code. Therefore, pull out your old scripts and find an effective way to obtain your output.

How to Compare Variables

To generate more accurate answers, you must know how to compare the values and specify what the interpreter must do based on the obtained result. Python allows you to use conditional statements to allow you to make these decisions. A conditional statement can transform the code or script from just being a list of instructions to a code that can be used by the user to make their own decisions. It would be useful to tell the interpreter to perform a different action as per the decisions made by the user. You can write pseudocode like:

if a specific condition is true:

then the following actions must be performed;

if another condition is true:

then these actions must be performed.

Each pair in the example above is a conditional statement, but before we learn more about these statements, let us take a look at how to specify these conditions. Different values can be compared using the following operators:

- <: Less than

- >: Greater than

- <=: Less than equal to

- >=: Greater than equal to

- ==: Equal to

- !=: Not equal to

These operators affect data types in different ways and give the user answers in the form of the Boolean operators. The data bits on either side of the operator are called operands, which are compared. The comparative operator and the operands together form the conditional expression. It is important to check the conditional statements or expressions you are using since you may obtain an error if you compare incomparable data types. The results obtained by comparing these numbers are self-explanatory.

>>> -2 < 5

True

>>> 49 > 37

True

>>> 7.65 != 6.0

True

>>> -5 <= -2

True

>>> 7 < -7

False

>>> 23.5 > 37.75

False

>>> -5 >= 5

False

>>> 3.2 != 3.2

False

Variables can also be used in conditional expressions.

>>> variable = 3.0

>>> variable == 3

True

Manipulating Boolean Variables

Before you move onto the different conditional structures used in Python, you must learn how to manipulate the Boolean values True and False. You can use these values to understand the characteristics of any variable. These operators are often used with the terms AND,

OR, and NOT. The statements below represent some bits of information.

>>> a = True

>>> b = False

>>> c = True

>>> d = True

>>> e = False

Let us take a look at how AND, OR, and NOT can be used.

>>> a or b

This operator returns the value True, since, for the OR operator, either one of the values needs to be true.

>>> c and e

This operator returns the value False since, for the AND operator, both values must be the same.

>>> not d

This operator returns the value False since the NOT operator provides the opposite of the value.

Combine Conditional Expressions

Conditional expressions can be combined to produce complex conditions that use the logical operators AND and OR. Let us take a look at the following conditions:

$(a < 6)$ AND $(b > 7)$

This statement will only return True if the value of a is less than six, and the value of b is greater than 7.

The Assignment Operator

Since you are familiar with the assignment operator (=), which you use to put a value into a variable, let us take a look at how you can use this operator to assign values to variables. This assignment operator can be used to unpack sequences.

>>> char1, char2, char3 = 'cat'

>>> char1

'c'

>>> char2

'a'

>>> char3

't'

The assignment operator can also be used to assign different variables with the same value.

a = b = c = 1

The assignment operator can also be used along with mathematical operators.

counter += 1

The statement above is interpreted as counter = counter + 1. Other operators also can be used to either increment or decrement the value of the variable.

How to Control the Process

You have the liberty to decide what happens next in the program you have written using a control flow statement. The results of the comparison statements can be used to create conditional statements that allow the interpreter to provide the output that is based on whether the predefined conditions hold true. Conditional statements can be constructed using the keywords if, elif and else. Unlike other languages, Python does not use the keyword then. The syntax is precise; therefore, you must pay close attention to the layout and punctuation.

if condition:

Perform some actions

print "Condition is True."

elif condition != True:

Perform some other actions

print "Condition is not True."

else:

Perform default or fall-through actions

print "Anomaly: Condition is neither True nor False."

In the syntax above, the first line begins with the word if, which must be followed by a conditional statement that gives a True or

False output followed by the colon. This colon means yes. The statements that follow must always start on a new line. You can leave as many spaces as you would like in a line of code, but it is important to ensure that the code that is written after the colon follows the same rules of indentation. It is always a good idea to use the right number of spaces across the code since it will help you control the flow of the program throughout your code. The group of statements that are written after the colon constitute a suite.

You can also include some conditional sections to your code using the elif keyword. This keyword is the abbreviation of the conditional statement else if which cannot be used in Python. You must remember that the statements under the elif section are evaluated only if the condition in the previous section fails. We will learn more about this later in the book.

You are also allowed to include a final else statement, which will then look at any value for which the condition did not hold true. This section does not make any statements or conditions. You can use this to specify the default set of actions that you can perform. In the previous example, there will be an error if the conditions in the if and elif statements are not clearly defined.

You can nest statements if you wish to include more possibilities, and you can ignore the usage of the elif statement entirely. You should do this only when you do not want any action to be performed if the condition held true. In simple words, there are times when you want some action to be only performed when the condition holds true, but not when the condition is false.

Make sure that the indentation goes back to the same level once you have written the final statement in your code. This will let the interpreter know that the conditional block of code has ended. The interpreter can only know if a block of code has ended based on the indentation, and it cannot use punctuation marks like other languages to mark the block of code. This makes it important for you to maintain your indentation across the script. The interpreter will throw an error if you have not maintained the indentation across your script.

```
>>> if c:

print(c)

c += 1

indent = "bad"

File "<stdin>", line 4

indent = "bad"

    ^
```

IndentationError: unindent does not match any outer indentation level

A conditional statement always gives the user the ability to check or validate the data used as the input. Validation is often performed when the data is first fed into the computer. Data is also validated before it is written as an output on a database record or file.

How to Deal with Logical Errors

You will need to develop formal ways to test your script as the applications you are developing become more complex. You can construct a trace table to make it easier for you to do this. You must trace the values of all the variables and the conditional expressions throughout the execution of the program.

You should perform a trace with different sets of data to ensure that any alternative is tested across the entire script. The errors in a program will never occur if the values that are being tested will lie within some range. The errors do occur for critical or unusual values. A critical value is any value in the script that will always lie outside of the tolerance of the interpreter or the program. For example, the program may not have the ability to work with a specific number. We need to work these out earlier during the design process to ensure that a program can be tested properly. In the calculation of the area of a triangle, the value taken into account is the breadth, which is set at 14 cm. Allowing 8 cm means that the maximum breadth of the triangle can only be 8 cm.

Using the Conditional Code

You can now apply your understanding of different conditional statements to measure the material that you have in your data set. If the breadth of the triangle were too much, it would become a different type of triangle. Therefore, you need to identify the right code that reflects the right conditions. The first step would be to translate your trace values into pseudocode. The following example is about measuring the length of a curtain.

if curtain width < roll width:

total_length = curtain width

else:

total_length = curtain length

if (curtain width > roll width) and (curtain length > roll width):

if extra material < (roll width / 2):

71

width +=1

if extra material > (roll width / 2):

width +=2

Loops

While Statement

result = 1

while result < 1000:

result *= 2

print result

You can control the number of times that you process a loop by using conditional statements in the loop. The loop will continue to run if the conditional statement written at the start of the loop will hold true at the beginning. In the previous example, the result of our conditional statement is greater than 1000. The loop will continue to process as long as the value of the variable is less than 1000. If the result reaches 1024 (2^{10}), the loop will stop functioning and will end. The variables used in the condition of the loop are expendable in the sense that they do not have to be used anywhere else in the code. You can name the integer counter as i or j instead of assigning some names to the variables.

There are two things that you will need to remember when you are constructing any code. A variable that is used in a conditional statement should always be initialized before the loop is executed. There should also be a way to update the expressions in the conditional statement. The loop will go around and around forever, which is called an infinite loop.

You can use different types of variables in the conditional expression that you write. Let us look at a problem where you are required to calculate the average of numerous inputs made by the user. The issue with this is that you never know how many numbers can be used as an input in the statement. The only solution here is to use a sentinel value, which will help you control the loop. Instead of using a counter, you can instruct the interpreter to look at the value that has been entered by the user. If the number entered is positive, the loop will continue to process, but the loop will be broken if the value entered is negative.

Let us take a look at the following example:

```
counter = 0

total = 0

number = 0

while number >= 0:

number = int (input ("Enter a positive number\nor a negative to exit: "))

total += number

counter += 1

average = total / counter

print(average)
```

There are numerous ways in which you can exit a loop cleanly. You can use the continue and break keywords for the same purpose. If you want to exit a loop and stop executing any statements in the body of the loop, you should use the break keyword. If you want to iterate a specific part of the loop, you should use the continue statement. This will help you execute that section of the loop that you want to execute.

There are times when you will need the interpreter to recognize the condition and not perform any other action. You can use the pass keyword in this instance. This keyword will create a null instance that will

There are times when you want to instruct the interpreter to do nothing if a condition holds true. In this instance, you can use the pass keyword. This keyword will create a null statement that will instruct the interpreter to only move to the next instruction in the code.

Nesting Loops

It is easy to nest conditional statements and loops in Python, and you can create an infinite loop, but it is important to remember to keep the number of levels to a minimum. It is easy to get confused about the option that the interpreter is currently using. It also makes it difficult for people to read the code since there will be multiple indentations in your code. It is possible that the nesting also slows down the execution of the program. In simple words, this is the wrong way to write your program.

If you write a code that has over three layers of looping, you should redesign the code so you can avoid making too many errors.

For

You should also have a good understanding of the 'for' control flow statement. This statement is written in the same way as the if and the while statements. The syntax is written as the keyword followed by a suite of instructions that have been indented well. The loop variable element will contain the first element in the sequence during the first iteration of the loop. The statements within the suite can now use this variable. During the second iteration, the variable takes the second element, and so on.

If you want to learn more about this statement, you should understand sequences. A simple example of a sequence in Python is a string. A string is a sequence of characters that include punctuation and spaces. Tuples and lists are other types of sequences that can be used in Python. A tuple and list are a sequence of items, and as mentioned earlier, a list can be edited once created while a tuple cannot. You can construct them in a statement in the following manner:

```
# tuple

sequence1 = (1, 2, 3)

# list

sequence2 = [1, 2, 3]
```

Chapter Ten

Data Structures

In the last few chapters, you learned how you could work with individual pieces of data to obtain some simple results. Real-world data is usually available in groups or lumps, and it is easier to work with groups since it makes it easier for us to eliminate repetitive code. Numerous data types in Python will make it easier for you to handle large groups of data.

Programmers often use strings, lists, dictionaries, and tuples when they write a script in Python. These data types are known as data structures. Strings are pieces of text that are grouped, while tuples and lists are groups of individual data items that have been grouped. A dictionary is a group of pairs that have the highest considerations. The different methods that are used to access the data in these structures are the same. This will be covered in detail in later parts of the chapter.

You can also look at these data types differently, depending on whether the values that the variable holds can be modified. This is called the mutability of the data type. A string and tuple cannot be modified, but they can be used to create new tuples and strings. A list is mutable, which means that you can either remove or add items to it.

Items in Sequences

You can fetch individual items in a sequence using an index. This index will indicate the position of the element. The index is often an integer that is written in square brackets immediately after the name of the variable. So, you can obtain the variable in a list by specifying the name of the list, followed by the index. You can also access a single character in a string.

>>> vegetable = 'pumpkin'

>>> vegetable [0]

'p'

Or an item in a list:

>>>vegetable = ['pumpkins', 'potatoes', 'onions', 'eggplant']

>>>vegetable [1]

'pumpkins'

You will notice that indexing in Python is zero-based. This means that you can only start counting the variables at zero. An index with the number 3 in the square brackets will look at the fourth item in the list since the first item will be indexed as zero. So, you can use any number of integers beginning from zero to index the variables in your data set. A negative index will count the list from the end to the beginning:

>>>vegetable [-1]

'eggplant' Slices can be used to grab the different sections in any sequence. This method is used to fetch many items in a sequence. A slice is written using the same notation as an index. The only difference is that a colon separates the integers. The first value is the starting point, and this value is included. The second number in the notation is the endpoint of the slice, and it is exclusive. If you look at s[0:2], the compiler will slice the list from the variable with the index zero and stop exactly before the variable with the index two.

You do not necessarily have to use the third value, and this is an additional step. This can be negative; therefore, you can retrieve all the other items instead of picking this item from the sequential list. Alternatively, you can retrieve items backward as well. So, s [i: j: step] will give you the slice that begins from the variable i, but will not include the variable j. Here, s is the sequence.

If you ignore the initial point, the slice will always start at the beginning of the sequence. If you forget the end, the slice will continue to the end of the original or main sequence.

Slicing and indexing do not change the original sequence. They will develop a new sequence. The actual data items in the sequence will be the same. So, if you want to modify an individual item in the sequence, you will see that the item has changed in the slice as well.

Tuples

Tuples are a group of items or elements that are ordered and immutable. You should think of a tuple as a sealed packet of information.

A tuple is specified as a comma-separated list of values. These values can be enclosed within parentheses if necessary. In some cases, these parentheses are required, so always use them regardless of whether or not you think they are necessary. The values in the tuple do not necessarily have to be of the same data type. Some values can also be other tuples.

Creating a Tuple

Tuples can be created with no items in it using the round brackets ().

>>>empty_tuple= ()

If you do not want more than one item in the tuple, you should enter the first item, followed by a comma.

>>>one_item = ('blue',)

Changing Values in a Tuple

The values in a tuple cannot be changed. These tuples are sealed packets of information that are often used in situations where a set of values need to be passed on from one location to another. If you wish to change the sequence of the data, you should use a list.

List

A list is a comma-separated and ordered list of items that are enclosed within square brackets. The items within the list do not have to be of the same data type. You can also include a list within a list.

A list can be concatenated, indexed, and sliced just like any other sequence you can use in Python. You can change some items within a list when compared to a tuple or string. Lists are very flexible when compared to tuples. You can either clear a list or change the list completely by slicing the list and assigning the data to other variables.

Creating a List

It is easy to create a list.

>>> shopping_list = ['detergent', 'deodorant', 'shampoo', 'body wash']

Modifying a List

A new value can be added to a list using the assignment operator.

>>> shopping_list [1] = 'candles'

>>> shopping_list

['detergent,' 'candles,' 'deodorant,' 'shampoo,' 'body wash']

Stacks and Queues

You can use lists to store and retrieve data or variables in a specific order since lists are ordered data types. The main models that one can use to do this are by using stacks and queues. A stack uses the last in first out (LIFO) approach. A real-world example of this approach is how the discard pile is used in a card game. You add cards to the top of the pile and remove the card from the top. You can include items into a stack using the list.append() function and remove the items from a stack using the pop() function. There are no additional index arguments that you will need to include when you use these functions, so the last item in the list is removed.

>>> shopping_list.append ('brush')

>>> shopping_list.pop()

'candles'

>>> shopping_list

['detergent,' 'deodorant,' 'shampoo,' 'body wash']

The second approach is to create the first in first out (FIFO) structure. A queue uses this type of approach. This method works like a pipe where the first item is pushed out of the pipe before the remaining items. You can use the same functions, append() and pop(), to either push items into the queue or remove them from the queue. You will, however, need to use the index zero to indicate that the items should be popped from the start of the list.

>>> shopping_list.append ('brush')

>>> shopping_list.pop(0)

'detergent'

>>> shopping_list

['deodorant,' 'shampoo,' 'body wash,' 'brush]'

Dictionaries

A dictionary is much like an address book. If you know the name of the person you wish to contact, you can obtain the details of that person. The name of the person is the key, while the details of the person are the value.

The key that you use in a dictionary should be an immutable data type; that is, it can be a number, tuple, or string. The value can be anything. A dictionary is a mutable data type, and it is for this reason that you can add, modify or remove any pairs from the dictionary. The keys are mapped to an object, and it is for this reason that a dictionary is also known as mappings. This will show you that a dictionary behaves different to a sequence.

A dictionary can be used anywhere you want to store a value or attribute that will describe an entity or a concept. For instance, you can use a dictionary to count the number of instances of a specific state or object. Since every key has a unique identifier, you cannot have duplicate values for the same key. Therefore, the key can be used to store the items in the input data, and the values can store the result of the calculation.

Chapter Eleven

Working with Strings

Commands used in Python 3 work in the same way as commands in Python 2. There are a few important changes that you need to keep in mind. The most significant change is how the string data type can be used. In earlier versions of Python, the string data type was coded as a single sequence of bytes using the ASCII character set. This set was used to represent the text.

To make changes to the string type, the print statement in Python 2.x has been replaced with the print() function, which is a built-in function in version 3.0. This function replaces most of the earlier syntax with keyword arguments. If you want to balance this, you should replace the input() function using the raw_input() function. You should also use the function eval(input()) in the same way you would use the old input() function.

Splitting Strings

Since strings cannot be changed, that is, they are immutable; you may want to split them into smaller variables or lists to make it easier for you to manipulate the content. It is important to remember that a delimiter is a string of characters or a character that is used to separate a unit of data or words. The list can be split numerous times using the maxsplit() function, and you will end up with maxsplit+1 lists. If you do not specify a separator, the string will only be split using whitespaces.

```
>>>sentence = 'This is a long sentence'

>>> sentence.rstrip('sentence').split()

['This,' 'is,' 'a,' 'long']
```

You can split a string using the string.partition(sep) function, which will return the tuple (head, sep, tail). When you use this method, the interpreter identifies the separator within the string and then returns the section before the separator and the part of the string that is separated from the string. If the interpreter cannot find the separator, the method will return two empty strings and the original string.

Concatenation and Joining Strings

You can use the plus operator if you want to combine strings, but this is a very inefficient way of doing it. When you combine the plus operator with different print functions, it will slow the execution of your program. Python is not slow, and it is often better to manipulate the list of words in a statement and then use the function string.join(sequence) to return the value of a string, which is a combination of the strings present in a sequence. This method is the exact opposite of the string.split() function. The data that you wish to manipulate is present in the sequence of the argument, and the string that you wish to use is the string of characters you want to use to separate the items in the string. The value could either be an empty string or space.

```
>>> s1="example"
>>> s2 = "text"
>>> s3 = " "
>>> s3.join([s1,s2])
'example text.'
```

You must remember that the function string.join() always expects a sequence of strings as the argument.

>>> s3 = "-"

>>> s3.join ('castle')

'c-a-s-t-l-e'

You also may need to convert different data types into strings by using a sub list.

Editing Strings

You cannot edit a string in a few places alone, but there are some methods that you can use to edit strings. These methods will return new versions of the string.

There are times when you will need to remove the whitespaces at the beginning of the end of the string. This will need to be done if you are trying to work on comparing the user input with any other value that is stored in the system. You can do this by using the string.strip([chars]) method. The method will return the copy of the string by removing all the characters at the beginning and the end of the sequence. If there are no arguments given to the string, the function string.strip() can be used to remove these whitespaces.

>>> sentence = 'This is a long sentence'

>>> sentence.strip('A')

' This is a long sentence.'

How to Match Patterns

There are times when you cannot use basic string methods. For instance, you may have to retrieve the values that are present in a regular pattern in a block of text, but you never know what these values will be. This is when you will need to use a regular expression. A regular expression or regex for short is a pattern that can be used to match some text in your code. In the simplest form, a regular expression is a plain string of characters that match itself. The regular expression will use a syntax that has some special characters. These characters can be used to recognize a wide range of possibilities that can be matched. You can also use these expressions in search and replace operations and also split the text up in numerous ways using the string.split() function.

A regular expression is complex and powerful and is often difficult to read. You can manage without using these expressions most of the time, but these expressions come in handy when you deal with some structured and complex pieces of text. It is always a good idea to take a regular expression slightly slowly, and learn them one at a time. When you try to learn the entire expression in one go, it can be pretty overwhelming. A regular expression matching operation is provided by the module 're.' This module is not a default module, and you will need to import it before you can use it.

>>> import rein

The module supports both 8-bit and Unicode strings, so it should be possible to recognize any characters that you can type in from the keyboard or read from a file.

Next, you need to construct a regular expression string to represent the pattern you want to catch. Let's use the rather colorful string from earlier in the chapter again.

Chapter Twelve

Working with Functions

When you create a new function, you will need to understand the type of input that the function will need and what information it will return. It is also important to identify the structure and the type of data that you will be feeding into the function. The data that is given to a function is termed as the parameter, and the information returned by a function is known as the output or the result. The initial specification for any function design should include the general description of the specific purpose of the function.

Defining a Function

A function is always defined using the def statement. The function name follows the word def, an optional list of parameters, and the line ends with a colon, which indicates that the subsequent lines should be indented as a suite or block of instructions. Let's start with a function that takes no parameters:

```
>>> def generate_rpc():

"""Role-Playing Character generator

"""

profile = {}
```

```
    print "New Character."

    return profile
```

This block of instructions proceeds in the same way as a complete script. So, in essence, we give a name to each piece of functionality, and they are called functions.

If you want to throw some light on the purpose of the function and what it does, you can do this in the docstring. This should be the first thing you look at when you write a function. The docstring will be followed by some statements that will explain the core functionality of the function and will be followed by the lines of code. You can use the function to return some value using the return statement.

In the above example, the last line of the function is used to specify the variables that will be returned to the main program. If you do not have to return anything, you can avoid using the return statement, and Python will assume that nothing should be returned to the main program. The block of code that you have written in your function has not been run yet but has been assigned to the definition of the function. You will need to call the function in the main program to run the code.

Since we have given names to functions, we can call those functions any number of times:

```
>>> generate_rpc()

New Character

{}
```

In the above example, we have not specified any parameters, and it is for this reason that the parentheses after the function name are empty.

Defining Parameters

Most functions always work on some data that has been provided to them using the main program. If you want the function to receive the data, you will need to set up some containers that can hold the data. These containers will become variables that are always unique to the function and are known as formal parameters. It is always a good idea to ensure that these variables do not have the same name as other variables in the program. The formal parameters that you specify in the program will need to mention in parentheses once you define the name of the function in the first line of the definition.

```
Import random

def roll(sides, dice):

result = 0 for rolls in range(0,dice):

result += random.randint(1,sides)

return result
```

You can call this function from the main program using the following line of code:

```
muscle = roll(33,3)
```

The values in the parentheses are called arguments, and these arguments correspond to the formal parameters that can be found in the definition of the function. In the example above, the first argument being used is 33, and this argument is bound to the parameter sides. The second is three that is bound to the parameter dice. This will create two variables that can be used within the function. If you send values like this to the function, you will need to ensure that you have the same number of parameters and arguments. You can substitute the actual values that are present within the function using variables that you want. You must only remember that the function will refer to the value using the name of the parameter that obtains the value. The original variable will not be affected, and only its value is passed on to the parameter.

Documenting your Function

When you have written a function fully, and the script in the function will pass the tests that you have created for the code, you should begin editing the docstring to explain the use of the function.

You are required to follow some conventions when you are writing a docstring. The first line of the docstring should be concise and should describe the function that is being used. This statement should make sense by itself. The second line of the docstring should always be left blank. The body of the docstring should contain an explanation of the parameters within the function, some details about the function, an explanation of the algorithm used and an example of how you can use the function including some information about keyword arguments, optional variables and the values that the function will return.

You can also choose to include some information about some errors or exceptions one may encounter. You can also talk about some of the restrictions on the function. In short, the information that the programmer will need to know to understand the function better should be present in the docstring. You must remember to update the comments and the docstring every time you make a change to the code.

Working with Scope

It is easier to look at a function as a black box that takes in some data, processes that data, and returns the required values to the user. The code written in the main section of the program will send the source data and receive the results. This code is known as the calling procedure. This procedure does not need to know the data that is present in the black box, as long as the source data, and the results have been identified clearly.

Understanding the Scope

You never have to worry about naming a function when you are writing your program. We have the concept of scope only to cater to this purpose.

When you run a program in Python, the interpreter will create a list of the names being used in the program and will keep track of those names. The names are placed in a table called the symbol table and will be used by the interpreter as the dictionary. The variables that are created in the symbol table of the program are known as global variables since any part of the program can access these variables. These variables can be viewed using the globals() function. The result of running globals() is the same as the result of running vars() without including any arguments. The scripts that we have looked at in the book only use global variables.

A variable that is created within a function will be stored in the symbol table. These variables are unique to the function alone. The data is known as local data and can only be accessed using the locals() function. The main body of the program will not allow you to access variables that are set in the function. The function will still be able to access the variables in the main program. This means that you have two ways to process data in a function. The easiest way to do this is to take the data that you want to use as a parameter for your function. The function will process that data and return the required result. The main program will then use this result. The other way is to allow the function to access any global data and process it as required. It is best not to use this method since the function will only work with specific variables names, and cannot be used anywhere else.

Manipulating Dictionaries and Lists

Every parameter to a function is passed using a value. In the case of an object, which is different from a string or an integer, any changes made to the object are reflected outside of the function as well. This means that a function can always be used to modify mutable data types like lists or dictionaries. A pure function is often not used to perform any modifications to the data since the function will not return any value or use any input parameters.

If you want to avoid any effects of using a mutable function, it is always a good idea to only use or return immutable values in a function. You should always keep the modification procedures separate. If you send a dictionary or a list to any other function, you are only sending the value to a pointer that will have the same global instance for the object as if you had written local_list = global_list.

Abstraction

You will identify some new issues when you work on this aspect of testing. If you want to keep track of what is happening with your code, you must write the minimum necessary code to ensure that the code passes the test. If the new code fails, you must roll all the changes back to the point where the code will pass the test. If you use a function that does not work, you should not worry too much about it. All you need to do is reverse the changes that you have made and move to the next section of your code. There is no rule which states that everything that you write in a program should be placed within a function.

Abstraction is the process of shifting chunks of code into a function and turning the code that deals with a general idea into a smaller section of code that can be used anywhere within the script. Once you create functions, you can move them outside the code and call upon them whenever necessary, and it is for this reason that abstraction is a good method to use in your code. The only rule that you need to keep in mind is that you should always write the test code first and ensure that it passes through the interpreter before you refactor it. This approach will seem difficult, but it is the best way to develop new code with no errors. You can focus on writing newer pieces of code instead of worrying about the details of the code.

Chapter Thirteen

Introduction to Data Mining

Data mining is an analytical process that you can use for your business to convert raw data into relevant information that you can use. By using specialized tools, you can detect patterns in large-scale information to learn more about your customers and, in response, develop more effective strategies. The goal is to decrease your expenditures and increase your revenue. Effective data mining relies on efficient data gathering and storage, as well as analytical processing.

Retail shops, such as grocery stores and supermarkets, are the most common users of data mining. Many retailers are offering loyalty rewards, which enable their customers to buy items at reduced prices or accumulate points. The loyalty cards could make it easier for these businesses to monitor that is purchasing what, the time that they are shopping it, and at what price margin. After doing some analysis, the business could use this information for several purposes, such as providing customer coupons targeted to their purchasing intent and deciding when to place items on sale or when to sell specific products at a higher markup.

Software

Software that is specially designed for data mining can analyze patterns and relationships in data according to the specifications requested by the business. For instance, data mining software could be used to develop classes of information. Let's say a grocery store likes to use data mining to identify the right time to offer certain products. It refers to the data it has captured and creates classes according to customer visits and what they have purchased. In some instances, data mining specialists may look for clusters of data according to logical relationships, or they study associations and patterns to make conclusions about consumer trends.

Strategies

Businesses can use different types of analyses to retrieve some valuable information from the data. Every type of business data analytics will have varying results or impacts. The type of data mining strategy you must use is dependent on the kind of business problem that you want to address.

Different forms of data analytics could result in different outcomes and thus offer different insights for the business. Among the most common ways to retrieve valuable insights is through the data mining process.

In developing your data analytics strategy, you must be clear on the definition of data mining and how it could help your business. You must remember that the most important goal of any process in data mining is to look for some relevant information that can be put in a database or warehouse. Let us look at some common types of data mining analytics that you can use for your business.

Association Analysis

Association analysis helps a business define and identify the associations between the numerous variables in the dataset. This data mining strategy enables you to identify the concealed patterns in your data set. You can use these patterns to identify the variables and all the occurrence of other variables in the data set that exist in different frequencies.

This data analytics strategy is often used by retail stores to look for some patterns in the information from POS. These patterns can then be used to recommend some new products to customers depending on their previous purchases. If you do this correctly, you can ensure that your customer conversion rate increases.

In the year 2004, Walmart used data mining to understand the sales pattern for different products, especially the Strawberry pops. This retail giant realized that the sale of Strawberry Pops always increased before a hurricane. Walmart then began to place this product near the checkout counter whenever there was a hurricane striking the area.

Anomaly Detection

Anomaly detection is a type of data mining technique where you look for variables in a dataset that do not match a predicted pattern or expected behavior. These anomalies are often termed as surprises, outliers, exceptions, contaminants, or extremes. That said, these variables offer some important information about the data set. An outlier is an object that can deviate from the average or the standard deviation of the variables in the data set. Outliers are always separate from the other data you have in the dataset, which means that they can signify that there is some inconsistency in the data or that the engineer or user needs to analyze the numbers.

You can identify frauds in a system using anomalies in the data set. These variables will have a distinct set of characteristics that will help you determine the outcome of the data set. Businesses can use this method to identify those areas in their business where the processes are flawed. They can also use these methods to identify any fraud in the business. It is important to remember that in a large-scale data set, there will be a small number of anomalies. These variables may show some bad data, but these can also be present in the data set because of a variation in the data set. These variables can also show that there is something impressive about the data set. It is in these situations that you will need to perform more analysis.

Regression Analysis

You can identify the dependency of different variables or attributes in the data set using regression analysis. There is an assumption that one variable can affect the response of another variable. Independent attributes can be affected by another attribute, but this does not mean that there is some form or level of dependency. You, as a business owner, can identify whether the variables in the dataset are dependent on one another or not.

Regression analysis can help businesses identify the different levels of customer satisfaction or determine the number of clients the business has. Businesses can also use this analysis to see how a change in the business structure will affect customer loyalty. The business can also understand how the different service levels can be affected because of some external factors.

Every dating website uses regression analysis to offer better services to the members. Almost all websites use regression analysis to help two members connect based on their attributes. Tinder is a classic example, where you only receive notifications about people who have similar hobbies and habits.

Data mining and science can be used by businesses to identify the right information and focus on that information to develop models. These models can then be used to make projections on how people or systems will behave. You can build better models if you gather more data.

Classification Analysis

Classification analysis is a technique where you need to gather some relevant and crucial information about different variables and factors. This type of data mining analytics can help a business identify which data set it will need to use to perform further analysis. Businesses often use classification analysis against cluster analysis, since classifying the data is a pre-requisite for the clustering algorithm.

Email providers often use classification analysis to classify the email that any user receives as spam or useful. This can be done using data that is present in the email; for example, the algorithm can use the files attached in the email to define whether the email is useful or not.

Clustering Analysis

Clustering analysis is another data mining process that refers to the process of identifying the data sets that have some similar attributes and using those attributes to learn the similarities and differences in the data. Clusters have some specific traits which an engineer can use to enhance the algorithm to improve targeting. For example, clusters of customer information that talks about customer purchasing behavior can be targeted to identify how the customer database would react to a change in products and services.

An outcome of clustering analysis is that you can develop some customer personas that you can identify a group of customers with. This will help you represent the customer types in a specific demographic. If you want to define these customer types, you should

98

always look at customer attitude or behavior and also identify the customers who are using your products and services. The business can use a particular software or programming language to work on relevant cluster analysis.

Chapter Fourteen

Data Visualization

"By visualizing information, we turn it into a landscape that you can explore with your eyes. A sort of information map. And when you're lost in information, an information map is kind of useful." – David McCandless

Here is a fun fact to start this chapter with. Ninety percent of the information that is transmitted to the brain is visual.

We have learned how data science is an essential platform that helps growth, development, and evolution of a business by helping it form and implement strategies using insights that are entirely driven by data. Data that is digital not only helps perceive essential insights to a business but if this data is presented in a manner that is digestible, inspiring and a logical format, it is like telling a story to everyone in an organization and getting them on board with your vision as a data scientist.

The part where we represent this data such that everyone in an organization who is not tech-savvy can understand too is the part where visualization of data comes into the picture. Visualization has a big part to play in data analytics and refers to the creation of graphical representations. This whole process of data visualization helps interpret patterns in data by having a quick look at it and helps structure data in real-time while still preserving the backend data, which is complex owing to its factual and numerical figures.

Data interpretation is the biggest challenge in organizations that have huge sets of data readily available for analysis. Therefore, the aspect of data interpretation is very critical if we are looking at the goals, aims, and long term objectives of an organization.

This is where data visualization comes into the picture.

The human brain can remember visuals way more comfortably as compared to numbers and letters. Therefore, the representation of data that is huge and complex in the form of graphs or charts is more convenient as compared to reports or spreadsheets.

Critical aspects and concepts of data can be conveyed in a simple, intuitive, and swift manner with the help of visualization techniques. Visualization also helps data scientists to do experiments with data based on different scenarios by allowing them to make tiny adjustments.

The visualization of data has proved to be very beneficial to organizations. It has been observed that business meeting durations can be lowered by 24 percent if data is represented in a visual format as compared to raw data. Another study shows that with the use of visualization techniques, return on investments for a business could be increased to USD 13.00 for every dollar that is spent.

It can, therefore, be concluded that business success rates can improve tremendously with the aid of visualization techniques, and a business can yield a value which is optimum by using this technique that has already been tried and tested to achieve results. Let us go through the essential techniques that are available for data visualization in the industry today.

Know your Audience

The concept of knowing your audience is the most overlooked of all and yet is one of the most vital concepts in data visualization.

We can safely assume that the world wide web, the Internet, and information technology as a whole are still in its infant stages. Furthermore, we can safely assume that data visualization is even a far younger concept in comparison. Even the most established entrepreneurs of the 21st century sometime find it difficult to understand one single pie chart or a neatly presented set of visuals, or mostly do not have the time to sit through and deep dive into the data available even via graphical representations. Therefore, it is imperative that the data that you are converting into a visual format is interesting and tailored to suit the audience that you are presenting it to. This is why it is essential to know your audience before you put forth a set of visual data in front of them.

Set your Goals

As with many businesses, right from the storytelling of your brand to sell your products digitally and beyond, visualization of data and your efforts will only yield if the strategy behind your business is concrete. At the time when you are creating a visualization of data for your business, the visuals must show a logical narrative and insights that are most relevant to your business. By creating a goal for your pursuits or campaigns, you should sit down with all the stakeholders and explain your goals to them until they are as invested as you are in your goals and dreams. One of the ways of achieving this is by setting KPIs for your business that is predetermined and uses these KPIs as an input to your visualizations.

Choose the Right Type of Charts

Selecting the right kind of charts to represent your data plays a significant role. Therefore, it is very critical to select the right type of charts to represent your data effectively, all while keeping in mind the project in concern, the purpose of the project, and the audience.

For example, if the project is showing changes that happened over various periods for business and shows only a few insights, using a simple line graph or a bar graph would be the most optimized technique of representing data visually.

Let us go through the most popular chart types that are used to represent data visually.

Number Charts

Number charts are very efficient and effective when the data is supposed to show an indicator that is of key performance such as site visits for a website, likes on a picture on Instagram, or even sales KPIs of a company.

Maps

The most significant advantage of using maps is that they are fun to look at, which means that the audience that the map is being presented to (such as a board panel or presentation) will be highly engaged. The second advantage is representing data using maps is easy and quick, and large sets of complex data on information of geography or other things can be easily digested when shown using maps.

Pie Charts

Pie charts have been considered to be the most traditional way to represent data and have received a lot of negative feedback in recent years. We still feel that pie charts are an excellent tool for the visualization of data and are easy to follow.

Gauge Charts

Data that has single values or data points can be efficiently represented using gauge charts. Gauge charts are one of the best visual representations to display an instant indication of trends, whether it be dashboards used in financial organizations or for executive dashboard reports.

The Color Theory Advantage

This is the most straightforward and basic technique which is to be taken care of during data visualization - a selection of a color scheme that is appropriate and relevant to the data such that it significantly enhances your efforts.

The color theory plays an essential part in making your visualization model success or a failure. Consistency is the key, and you should always maintain a scheme that is consistent across your models. You should distinguish elements in your models by using clear contrasting color schemes. (example: negative trends in red and positive trends in green).

Handling Big Data

It is estimated that by 2020, there will be 1.7 megabytes of data that will be generated every second for every human that exists on the planet. This can be overwhelming and will deliver great insights in the digital world that we are marching towards. It can be a real challenge to handle this data, interpret it, and present it whenever and wherever required. The following tips will help you learn how to manage the big data that is going to be generated.

1. There will be a lot of data available, and you will need to decide how much of this data holds value for you or your organization.

2. To ensure that data is managed smoothly across all departments, you need to ensure that all your colleagues and other people working on your project know your sources of data.

3. Always protect your data and keep your data handling systems simple such that they can be converted into visuals comfortably, and everyone finds it easy to understand.

4. Business dashboards should be easy to access and must show all the valuable insights into your projects.

Prioritize using Ordering, Layout, and Hierarchy

Following up on our discussion of the previous topic, after you have categorized your data based on how much of it is valuable to your organization, the next step should be to dig further and creating a hierarchy in your data by labeling it. You should prioritize your data by using something like a color code based on how vital a set of data is. This will help you to assign a visualization model to every data set based on its importance, and that will bring out the best out of every visualization model.

Utilization of Network Diagrams and Word Clouds

Network Diagrams or Word Clouds come handy when you are dealing with the visualization of data that is unstructured or semi-structured.

When you need to draw the graphical chart of a network, a network diagram is used. This technique is usually used by designers, network engineers, data analysts, etc. when they need to compile network documentation in comprehensive formats.

On the other hand, complex data consisting of unstructured information can be presented in an efficient manner using word clouds. In contrast with a network diagram, a word cloud is an image that is created using words that are used for a particular subject or text. The size of that word represents the importance and frequency of each word.

Comparisons

This is a data visualization technique that is very brief, but it is still important, according to us. Comparison, as many as possible, should be put forward whenever you are presenting your insights and information. You can show the same information over two different timeframes and draw comparisons between them using two or more graphs. This helps drill down the information deep into the brains of the audience that you have, and they will remember it.

Telling a Story

As one may see in content marketing, even when it comes to presenting data in front of an audience, you should make it feel like telling a story of how the data originated and then evolved further and how it will eventually prove to be beneficial to the organization. Observation shows that an audience stays more focused and engaged when a presentation is done in the form of a story.

Chapter Fifteen

Data Integration

Data integration refers to the process of combining data from independent sources, which are warehoused using different tools and usually offer a single perspective of data. Integrating data is crucial in the case of merging two businesses or consolidating systems inside one company to get a single aspect of the data assets of the company.

Probably the most common step in data integration is to set up the data warehouse. The advantage of a data warehouse is that it will enable a business to conduct analyses according to the data inside the warehouse. This may not be doable on data available on different source systems because such systems may not have the required data, although the data sets may be named similarly.

Moreover, if you want to keep data integration solutions completely aligned with your business goals, then you have to be mindful of the particular kinds of business value that could result from the efficient use of tools and strategies for integrating data.

In this chapter, we will discuss the top ways that data integration can bring value to your business. There are several actual cases included in this chapter to show the various types of values that data integration can provide. Hopefully, this can help you explain to your partners or your boss the value of data integration. It could also serve you as a guide on how you can plan and design suitable data integration strategies to advance your business.

Value

Let us begin with a more generalized perspective of data integration. Most valuable data-driven practices in business often rely on one or several forms of data integration. There are business processes that cannot be functional without data integration. This is particularly true for data warehousing and business intelligence.

Remember, effective decisions may rely on calculated, aggregated, and time-bounded data sets within a data warehouse and this can never take place without effective data integration. Success in sales, for example, usually relies on a total view of every customer's information that is generally aggregated using tools and techniques for data integration.

Moreover, integrating various businesses, as well as their processes, using shared data, should be backed up by a data integration solution. This is helpful, whether the businesses are divisions inside one enterprise or different enterprises that can share data from one business to another. Meanwhile, business processes like just-in-time inventory or operational business intelligence should be backed up by an efficient data integration solution, which could be used in real-time or with a few delays.

As you try to advance your business, your pace will also accelerate. Data integration could speed up the process of gathering and integrating time-sensitive data at speeds that are not even possible a decade ago. Data integration and related business processes, such as data management and data quality assurance, can add value to business data. As a result, the value of business processes will also increase.

Identifying the Value of Data Integration

Identifying the business value of data integration once you see it can be more difficult than you might expect because this data analytics process is usually separated at a level or two from the systems that your business might be using. Nevertheless, in general, the data integration value is usually visible as valuable data. Below are common examples of data integration in this value field:

- A business executive who accesses a single view of customer information that was built with data integration through data sync.

- A business intelligence user enters a query into a data warehouse, after which the system responded with complete data models and metadata that were set up using data integration.

- Several business supervisors are accessing information on a computer that is updated in real-time or as needed through a data integration solution.

- A product supervisor who accesses a list of available supplies from a supplier within a data set, which the supplier established through data integration and delivered across business boundaries through the business-to-business exchange.

Even if data is accessible in a Graphical User Interface (GUI) or a report, business users may overlook that data integration provided the information. Many business executives fail to realize that data integration is responsible for collecting, preparing, and delivering most of the data that they may take for granted. Nowadays, data integration is a fast-changing discipline, which offers data for several types of applications, whether they are operational or analytical.

Benefits

The outcome of data integration is quite ubiquitous in the business world, which enables commercial activities. We often don't identify these activities to consider data integration as a crucial process in today's business.

If your business needs to confirm the value of data integration (a common requirement for sponsorship, investment, or approval for data integration), then you have to educate your partners or your boss about the critical role that data integration could play for your data-driven business processes.

Single, Unified View of Business Entities

Through data integration, the business can capture data from several sources to complete a single view of the entities of the business, such as assets, locations, staff, finances, products, and clients. This is on the same level of data warehousing, but this is more on operations and not on business intelligence.

By effectively using data integration, the business can complete its customer profile and improve value for any client-oriented business process, from sales and marketing to client support. Complete product data can also add value to business systems for procurement, product management, and supply chain manufacturing.

Data Warehousing and Business Intelligence

As a support system of data warehousing, data integration can add value to the business process. Through data integration, you can collect raw data from different sources and combine them to develop new products. A data warehouse will contain data and data sets that do not exist anywhere else in the business.

Moreover, because of the requirements of business intelligence, data that goes into the warehouse should be regularly reconfigured to develop calculated, aggregated, and time-bounded data, established into multichannel data sets. Data integration cannot collect data itself; instead, it can shift the data into these necessary structures.

Data integration for business intelligence will allow high-value processes. A data warehouse constructed through data integration allows decision making at the tactical, strategic, and operational layers. Data created through data integration is crucial to business intelligence strategies, such as dashboard reporting, performance management, advanced analytics, and online analytics. These data warehousing and business intelligence activities – also enabled by data integration – could help in customer retention, increase sales, improve the efficiency of business operations, guide sales, and marketing activities, enable strategic planning, and other valuable business outcomes.

Real-time Delivery of Data

Businesses need to adapt to the fast pace of the world, and data integration can help in integrating data at speeds that were impossible a decade ago. Real-time data delivery that is usually enabled by modern data integration systems can enable several high-value business processes.

Businesses are now using applications to monitor data, such as business activities, facility status, grid monitoring, and so on. These can be quite impossible without the real-time capacity for information delivery supported by data integration.

Operational business intelligence often captures data several times a day from operational applications and makes the data available for monitoring and other kinds of management or operational reports. This provides the business access to data for strategic and operational decision-making.

Data Integration Could Add Value to Business Data

Many business owners think of data integration as a process of moving data. Those who are trained in data science understand that it is not easy to move data around. There is a need to improve it. Every ideal data integration solution can add value to the process.

Data integration improves data during the process. Data quality strategies are being added to data integration solutions. This is organic because data integration could filter out concerns about data quality that should be fixed, as well as areas for improvement. Data integration can also help in improving metadata, data models, master data, and other attributes of data. Hence, the data could come out as complete, clean, and consistent.

Data integration can also help in building new databases that are valuable for the business. Remember that the data contained in the data warehouse can never be found anywhere else in the business. Similar to the value-adding system in manufacturing, data integration can capture raw materials and build them into new data sets.

Therefore, data integration can convert data to make it more valuable for more business processes. Aside from moving data, data integration can also convert data, so it is suitable for any target system. In simple words, data integration repurposes data, so more business units, as well as their processes, could be beneficial for the business.

Data Replication

Data replication, also known as data synchronization, is another data integration system that can help add value to any business. For instance, data replication may build a complete view of a central data hub for access by several users and applications. This is seen in central hubs for product data, customer data, and master data. Replication may also enhance relevant data across several applications, along with their databases. For instance, client-facing applications for contact centers can be limited to a partial view of a customer, unless a total view can be developed by replicating customer data across these applications.

Data's business value in replication is that more business owners have a more unified view of a separate entity, such as finances, customers, and products. Nevertheless, data replication systems may tend to move and integrate data more often – usually several times a day. This hastens the freshness or data currency in applications. Hence, data is not just complete but also updated, which is crucial for businesses that need current data for their decision-making.

B2B Data Exchange

B2B data exchange is a promising area for development because businesses can use data integration tools and strategies in areas where these could be rare. Many data exchanges are low-tech and manually entered, which should be replaced to be synchronized. Experts project a comprehensive modernization in data exchange between businesses, especially in product-centric enterprises like retail, suppliers, and manufacturing. This is also crucial for financial institutions, healthcare, and other organizations that are using procurement and supply chain systems.

The need to modernize data exchange between businesses is an urgent concern. There is also a need to develop business value in this area. In general, business partnerships are crucial to advance businesses in terms of market reach, revenue, and brand development. Business partnerships can grow by achieving better operational excellence through data integration.

Collaborative Practices

To ensure that data integration offers the best type of business value, the system must be aligned with the goals of the business that is relative to the data. Fortunately, several collaborative practices have emerged in recent years, so data specialists could easily streamline their work with a broad range of colleagues.

Collaborative Data Integration

Collaborative data integration is a loose strategy for coordinating the tasks of data integration teams, which include data specialists. In general, collaborative data integration uses applications and practices like code review, team hierarchy, project management, and software versioning.

Data Governance

Data governance refers to data integration processes that focus on privacy, security, risk, and compliance. Many businesses have expanded data governance to also cover quality, standards, architecture, and many other issues on data. The team working on data governance could help data scientists get a single view of business goals that are relevant to data and align their work correctly. Meanwhile, the change management process of data integration can enable data integration specialists to think of possible solutions to increase data value.

Unified Data Management

Unified data management is a recent business practice that aims to coordinate tasks across several data management disciplines described above. UDM also enables collaboration between business management and data management to ensure that most data management tasks add business value by supporting business management goals.

Data Stewardship

Data stewardship is designed for managing the quality of data by identifying and prioritizing the quality of work according to the needs of the business and certain parameters, such as technological capacity and budget. The person who is in charge of the data, also known as the data steward, should work together with business and technical people. Through the years, data integration specialists have used stewardship in their array of strategies for better credibility in the alignment and prioritization of data integration work.

Chapter Sixteen

Predictive Analytics 101

The field of predictive analytics is one that runs entirely on the data available. There can never be too much data. It is a good idea to have more knowledge about something. This will enable you to make more informed decisions (often more accurate). This is especially true when you need to make some predictions. When you have more information, the accuracy of the predictions you make will be higher. Consider the following example: you are on a game show. The game is straightforward and requires to pick one out of 5 doors. There is a reward only behind one door. The probability of you choosing the right door is 1/5. If you had any information regarding the doors and what lies behind them, you can make an educated guess, which would undoubtedly increase your chances of winning the prize. Predictive analytics is based on this idea of using data at your disposal to make predictions.

Exploring Predictive Analytics

If you were to know what the future holds for you for certain, you would start to lead your life very differently. How will your life change if you were to win the lottery next year? Ideally, you would begin to plan for your life ahead, and since you had the one year of planning, the odds are that you would lead a very peaceful life. By simply knowing something that would happen a year later, you would be able to live a much more efficient life. Predictive analytics allows you to do this to some extent (because you cannot tell for sure what will happen). Think about it this way - If you could forecast every moment in your life, you will learn to make the most of each moment. It could be considered to be somewhat of a superpower. You would be able to lead a successful and efficient life without ever running into any problems! This might sound a little dull to people who enjoy the adrenaline rushes of gambling and other uncalculated risks. People who are focused on being successful and rich would go to any length to have this ability. You will build on this ability when you work on predictive analytics.

Mining Data

In recent times, almost everyone in the world would have come across the term "big data." This means that there is too much data in the world, and it is true. We must learn to make use of the information that one can find out there.

Data is an extremely valuable asset for anyone. Many large companies around the world have special data analytics sectors so that they can acquire as much useful data as possible. The keyword here is useful. We need to be able to extract out of all the welter of data only that data which is relevant to us. This is called data mining. It is the procedure of finding patterns and traits in the data using machine learning algorithms. Then predictive analytics comes into play. You need to analyze the information to make educated predictions about future events. So, to summarize, we need to use data mining along with predictive analytics to extract value from a set of data.

Numerous companies across the globe that focus on data mining. The goal is to accumulate all the data, analyze it, and identify different methods that will help the business perform better than its competitors. This information also helps businesses optimize their operations. Companies also use this data to figure out how to expand their customer base and increase their market share in the process. How can they improve their stronghold in the marketplace? How can they use this data to enhance their competitive edge? Companies have been successful in figuring all of this out by using data mining and predictive analytics.

The tool of predictive analytics is not restricted to the sphere of the business alone. For instance, it has been employed by governments as well. Law enforcement agencies use this tool to figure out whether or not a person is a suspect. They track his movements and behavior and use this data to infer whether or not he is a criminal. Anti-terrorist organizations also use predictive analytics. They look at past data and try to make predictions about where the terrorists might attack next. Even sports organizations can use predictive analytics. A football coach may watch the tapes of his opponent to decipher the plays they run. This would put his team in a better position to win the game. Even students use predictive analytics, albeit on a smaller scale. When a big exam is coming up, students often look into the papers from previous years and try to predict what type of questions may be asked. This tool is in use in various spheres of life simply because any information about the future can put us in a much better position to make the most of it.

Highlighting the Model

Almost every phenomenon in the world has a mathematical model. These models are simply representations of the phenomenon. The advantage of models is that they can be used to investigate the phenomenon further and learn more about it. Consider a sales company. They will look to model the behavior of their customers. They accomplish this by emulating how the customers shop and browse through their webpage (if one exists). Some of the questions they use as building blocks to the model are:

- Have they read the reviews provided by users?

- The number of reviews read

- Whether both positive and negative reviews were read

- Were there any products they looked at before making a purchase?

- Did the customers purchase a product apart from the one that they were looking for?

- Did they view any pages before they made the purchase?

- Did they look at the products' descriptions?

The answers to all these questions are obtained from the analysis of past data. The company stores all the transactions and history of customers, and it uses different tools to identify patterns and trends which will provide answers to the above questions. The collection of the data is an important step, as well. Just collecting all the data and storing it will make the analysis extremely complicated. The company needs to set limits on the breadth and depth of data and the quality level. These limits will define the structure of the model and also the outputs expected.

The entire process of predictive analytics should not be confused with simply looking at the data and reporting whatever appears to the naked eye. These are just parts of the process of obtaining the data and extracting useful and important information from it.

Let us now come to the topic of how to approach any predictive analytics problem. It is advisable to follow a systematic procedure. This way, we will get the desired results from the process. The following are the steps involved:

1. Take time to understand the problem you are trying to solve completely. This understanding is fundamental.

2. Accumulate the relevant data and collate it so that examining it will become easier.

3. Now run data mining algorithms, machine learning algorithms, and other tools of statistical analysis on the data.

You should only look at that data, which is useful for the process. The data mining step is of utmost importance. Then you are required to run various algorithms on the data, which are step-by-step procedures that help you to arrive at a solution. The idea is to go through multiple combinations of data and try to answer several what-if scenarios. Build a mathematical model, run these algorithms, and use the answers to make the most of the future events.

For someone who has not used mathematical models ever, the question of what a model looks like arises. If you are familiar with programming terminology, you can use simple conditional statements. These statements could be used to instruct the machine to perform a specific function if something were to happen. If that doesn't happen, THEN do something else. Here is a simple example: If on a particular day, the market is up, then buy some shares of ABC. If at any point the stock is up by 10 percent, then sell the stock and earn the profits. Else, exit your position or wait until the stock goes up again.

Consider the example of an online shoe store. A model for this store could look something like this:

- If you see a user buy a shoe from one brand, you can recommend other products from the same brand.

- If you see a user purchase a shoe for a specific purpose (for example, casual, party wear, etc.), you can recommend other shoes that fit the purpose.

- If a user has purchased a pair of shoes, recommend those shoes that were purchased by other customers who have a similar taste. Adding Business Value

The competition in the business sector has been on the rise in the last few years. In such times, it is always incumbent upon the company to find new ways to outperform their competitors. Predictive analytics is a tool that can help companies achieve this goal. Companies can use data mining algorithms, machine learning algorithms, and other tools of statistical analysis to help them process large volumes of data. These algorithms will make it easier to extract the patterns and trends in the data set. Businesses that use these tools have a competitive edge in the market.

The usage of predictive analytics in making operational decisions can help increase the return on investment for a company. Companies will spend lesser time working with low impact and low-risk aspects and start focusing on the high impact and high-risk ones. For instance, almost all standard insurance claims can be paid out automatically. The claim will be flagged if the company uses a predictive modeling tool that can identify the outliers or any unusual claims. The company can then call upon the person responsible for the claim and take the necessary action.

As mentioned earlier, a company can use predictive analytics to predict future events. This way, the company can prepare for that event and put itself in an advantageous position to make the most of it. For example, a shoe company can increase the number of sports shoes in the store during the Soccer World Cup because the demand will increase. This way, they can cater to the demands of their customers and also have increased sales. The eighth law of data mining proposed by Tom Khabaza speaks about this as well. This law states that the value of any predictive model can be calculated based on two attributes:

- The accuracy of the prediction

- The new information provided by the model

- Endless Opportunities

Businesses want to use optimization algorithms to manage their inventories and allocation of resources among employees better. They want to make their planning process more dynamic. These companies are looking to pounce on opportunities and make the most out of them.

The use of predictive analytics can achieve all these goals. As explained in earlier sections, predictive analytics can be applied in various spheres ranging from business to sports organizations. Companies should invest in data mining and predictive analysis because if they do not, at least a few of their competitors will employ these tools and get ahead of them.

One of the greatest minds to have ever lived, Albert Einstein, once said, "Know where to find information and how to use it as that is the secret of success." This is the basic idea behind predictive analytics. The goal is to find information and use it to our benefit.

So, according to Einstein's quote, using predictive analytics will make you successful. You will need to use data mining, as well. Once you have the data you need, interpreting it is solely based on how good your knowledge of your field is. This knowledge is essential in finding valuable information in the data provided to you. Once you can correctly analyze your data and come up with predictions, you will become successful.

Empowering your Organization

The previous sections have discussed and concluded that predictive analytics would help make your company more successful. But how? The following are the three significant advantages provided by the use of predictive analytics.

Vision

The first advantage provided by the tool is the vision. Businesses can use these tools to look for patterns or trends that will give them a competitive edge in the market. It can yield results that can provide your company and insight into the future. This insight will help in preparing your company so that it can make the best of the future. This can help increase profits and also increase your customer base.

Predictive analytics will look through past data of your customers and can relate it to other data that exists. It will then look to assemble this data in a manner such that it can help solve problems. The following are some examples of how the tool arranges the data:

- Guessing your customers' next actions.

- Knowing your customers' wish lists.

- Categorizing your customers as loyal, seasonal, or wandering.

- Categorizing your customers and speculating about their needs.

Decision

There can be a bias when human beings decide to make decisions based on data. A predictive analytics model makes decisions that are free from bias and emotion. The model looks at past information and uses that data to make calculations and predictions. Hence, the results of a predictive analytics model are completely unbiased.

Banks also use predictive analytics for various reasons. One of the most common applications of the tool is for the banks to predict the creditworthiness of a person in the future. Based on this, banks decide whether or not to extend someone's credit or grant them a new credit card. If this were to be done by an employee of the bank, it would not be surprising to see that his decisions had some shades of bias in them.

Precision

Let us once again compare a person and a model working on predictive analytics. As mentioned earlier, one of the main steps is data mining. Data mining requires going through tons of data and picking out only the relevant data. There will be errors if a human being manually mines data since there is a lot of data for them to look at.

On the other hand, a model that uses a data mining algorithm will be able to achieve this goal faster and with more accuracy. Also, if you wanted it to be done manually, you would need to hire more than one person for the job. This way, you end up wasting resources as well. Hence, using automated tools for predictive analytics will help cut costs, reduce error, and also save time and resources. The precision that comes with using these automated tools gives rise to other benefits as well. For instance, if you were looking to launch a new product and wanted to know which customers to target. By using predictive analytics and looking at past consumer behavior, you can pick the customers you want to target, and this could lead to higher sales.

Starting a Predictive Analytics Project

Now that you know the advantages of using predictive analytics let us now talk about how to start your predictive analytics project. Let us keep all the arcane algorithms and math aside for a second. Humans have used predictions in many aspects of their lives for many years now. Weather forecasts are one of the most common examples. Even the common man uses prediction in daily life (remember the example of the student preparing for an examination).

If we want any accuracy out of these predictions, we will have to consider the past as well. Making predictions off the top of our heads without examining any data will rarely lead to any accuracy. You need to follow a certain procedure:

- Look through information and filter out the facts that are related to the problem

- Take your time to separate the current facts from the past facts

- After analyzing the data and looking for trends, try making predictions about what might happen

- Make multiple predictions and rank them in order of likeliness of occurrence.

This is where you can use predictive analytics. It can help you with each of the steps mentioned above. This way, you will have all the information you need about the problem at hand, which makes it easier for you to predict the outcome with higher accuracy.

When companies conduct predictive analysis, they use three key ingredients to arrive at their solutions:

- Business knowledge

- Data-science team and technology

- Data

Companies have the freedom to give more importance to one of the above factors when compared to others. A minimum focus on all three factors is essential to run successful predictive analytics.

Business Knowledge

The coach of a football team cannot become a coach without any knowledge of the sport. A Wall Street broker cannot become successful without any knowledge of the stock market. Similarly, for someone to run a predictive analytics project to fulfill some business needs, he needs to have some level of business knowledge. You cannot expect to obtain the desired results if you do not have the required knowledge. The leadership and management team of a company need to be well versed in the concepts of business.

It is important to ensure that the people using the tool to make decisions are willing to act. In a company, when someone presents an innovative idea, there needs to be a member of the management who believes in it and who will push for it. Similarly, the predictions made by the predictive analytics tool need to be adopted by the management, and this will only happen if they are ready to act upon those predictions.

The management and leadership team should also be held responsible for setting goals (quantifiable goals). Unless you can measure the outcome of the predictive analytics tool, you will not know if it is working as desired. Also, metrics will help keep employees determined to reach the goal. It gives them feedback as to whether or not they are doing what is expected of them.

Consult the stakeholders in the business. Generally, these are the people with the greatest knowledge in the field, and their advice can improve the functions of the tool. They will be aware of what patterns to look for. They will also provide information on which variables you should focus on when looking for trends. In case other variables need to be added to the model, the stakeholders will know which ones to pick. Finally, they can also look at the results of the tool and analyze them. Since they have a lot of knowledge in the field, they will be able to interpret the data accurately and will also be able to provide valuable predictions.

Data Science and Technology

The tools that you will use for predictive analytics should include at least 3 of the following four capabilities (all four would be advisable):

- Statistical analysis tools
- Machine learning algorithms
- Data mining
- Software used to build the model

As mentioned in the previous section, you want the decision-makers to be well versed in business concepts. They need not necessarily understand the technology that has been used for making the model. All they need to know is what the model is supposed to represent and have a good understanding of that. The data scientists (people who generate the model and conduct data mining) and the management should communicate regularly.

It is advisable to train the data scientists in the basic concepts of business. This will help them in generating a much more efficient model. Increased efficiency in the model can translate to better and more accurate results from the predictive analysis. Also, this basic knowledge will allow the data scientists to expedite the process. The model can be used to obtain results when it is developed fully. By collaborating with the management teams, data scientists will know if their model is working correctly. It is recommended that the data scientists know a little bit about business, and the management teams know a bit of data science.

An important stage in the process is the selection of the software for running the analysis. The following factors come into play at this stage:

- The complexity of data
- The source of the data
- The complexity of the business problem
- The variability of the data
- The cost of the product
- The people within the organization who will use the product

Data

The advantages that experience comes with cannot be overstated. When looking at two candidates for a job, you would certainly want to pick the one who has more experience in the field (assuming all other qualifications are equal). The same concept can be applied to an organization. If we look at an organization as a person, the amount of experience translates to the amount of data at the organization's disposal. With more data, you can perform a more thorough analysis and hence, more accurate results. Therefore with greater data, you can make more insightful decisions. It should now be evident that data is crucial in predictive analysis. Data helps in giving more effective results.

In its raw form, data poses several challenges. You must learn to pick the right data for your analysis. Data can be distributed across multiple sources, making it harder to accumulate. Sometimes data gets mixed with other third-party data, and this makes the segregation process complex. So, data scientists need to spend substantial amounts of time cleaning up the data and picking only that which is useful. You must look for extremities, duplicates, outliers, abnormalities, and missing data.

Big data also has some inherent qualities that can be very challenging. Some of these are volume, number of types, and variability. There is too much data that comes in too fast from different sources. All these qualities come together to make the job of data mining difficult. You need to remove important information from this cluster.

There are many algorithms that you can use to mine data. Which of these algorithms should you choose? The team responsible for data science needs to analyze the data and its type. Based on this, they need to select an algorithm that will best suit their needs. You should also ensure that you pay attention to the data set and choose the right algorithm for that data set.

Conclusion

Throughout the book, you have gathered information on what data analytics is and how you can use it to improve your decisions. I've detailed the importance of data and how it has changed the face of the world. I hope you gather the information necessary to help you make better decisions using the data collected..

References

https://www.simplilearn.com/data-science-vs-data-analytics-vs-machine-learning-article

https://www.analyticsinsight.net/five-ways-data-science-has-evolved/

https://www.dezyre.com/article/difference-between-data-analyst-and-data-scientist/332

https://www.scnsoft.com/blog/4-types-of-data-analytics

https://acadgild.com/blog/different-types-of-data-analytics

https://www.edvancer.in/common-types-data-science-techniques-must-know/

https://www.datapine.com/blog/data-visualization-techniques-concepts-and-methods/

https://visme.co/blog/examples-data-visualizations/

https://www.forbes.com/sites/bernardmarr/2017/07/20/the-7-best-data-visualization-tools-in-2017/#41ee204f6c30

https://mode.com/blog/python-data-visualization-libraries

https://datajobs.com/what-is-data-science

https://searchbusinessanalytics.techtarget.com/definition/big-data-analytics